Today

Today

Daily Meditations for Abundant Living

Simon Gibson

Inspirational Faith

Published by Inspirational Faith

Copyright © 2010 Simon J Gibson

All rights reserved. This publication may not be reproduced, stored in a retrieval system or transmitted, in any form or by any means, electronic mechanical, photocopying, recording or otherwise, without the prior permission of the publisher.

All Bible texts quoted are from the
New King James Version
unless otherwise stated.

ISBN 978-0-9562559-5-2

Visit us at

todayonline.biz

"He who desires to see the Lord within himself endeavours to purify his heart by the unceasing remembrance of God. The spiritual land of a man pure in soul is within him. The sun which shines in it is the light of the Holy Trinity. The air which its inhabitant breathes is the All-Holy Spirit. The life, joy and gladness of that country is Christ, the Light of the Light – the Father. That is the Jerusalem or Kingdom of God hidden within us, according to the word of the Lord. Try to enter the cell within you, and you will see the heavenly cell. They are one and the same. By one entry you enter both. The ladder to the Heavenly Kingdom is within you. It is built mysteriously in your soul."

St. Isaac the Syrian

Contents

	About This Book	9
1	Today	11
2	Prayer for the Day	23
3	The Meditations	37
	January	39
	February	57
	March	73
	April	91
	May	107
	June	125
	July	141
	August	159
	September	177
	October	193
	November	211
	December	227

About This Book

If, like me, you want to live your life to the full, this book is written for you. It's a book about today and how to make the most of it. At its heart is the timeless principle that truly abundant living is found in a personal relationship with God, and nowhere else.

This is a book of daily meditations. When you wake, you wake to a new day. What will you make of it? Will you spend it in peace or in fear, in faith or in despair, in love or in hate? Each meditation is written to help you live each day to the full.

How do you see each day? Your view of the day will significantly influence your experience of it. See each day in the light of Heaven, and you will discover the right path to take. Face each day in the strength of God, and you will be ready to seize its opportunities and meet its challenges. Live each day by faith, and you will have power to live victoriously through both the good times and the bad. Chapter One will help you establish such a mind set, and position you for for daily success, Heaven's way.

How do you begin each day? If you want to make the most of every day, you need to start it well. Chapter Two contains a simple but highly effective way of ensuring that you live every day to the full.

What do you read each day? There is no greater book than the Bible, and no greater news than its message from Heaven. Open the Bible, and you open a window through which the Light of Eternity floods your soul with wisdom, love, and power. Apply its truths, and your life will be supernaturally changed for good. Chapter Three, the major part of this book, contains meditations and Bible readings for each day of the year.

If you do not know God, I pray that by reading this book, you will find Him. If you know Him, but would walk with Him more closely, I pray that this book will help you to hear from Heaven more clearly, more fully, and more consistently, than ever before. Seek Him daily, and you will learn to discern His voice, follow His directions, and abundantly fulfil your unique calling in life.

There is only one 'today', and that's the day you are in. Make it count!

Simon Gibson 2010

1
Today

How do you see each day?

How you see today is important. What do you say to yourself when you wake up? You may or may not realise it, but your waking thoughts can make or break the day ahead. It is as though they set the stage for what is to follow.

From the moment you wake, your thoughts are beginning to shape your experience of the day. These waking thoughts can exert a profound influence, not only on how you will experience the day as it unfolds, but also on the decisions that you will make during it.

Some people say on waking, "Oh no, another day!" Others find themselves dwelling negatively on the problems, difficulties, and challenges that they are currently facing. Neither is a recipe for a good day. In fact, such negative perceptions are more likely a recipe for painful feelings of fear or anxiety, anger or frustration, guilt or failure, sadness or depression.

Although it is true that we are the victims of our own unhelpful thinking, it is also the case that we may choose to think better thoughts. To a large degree we are responsible for the thoughts that we think, and these have the power to transform our lives for good or for ill. As the writer of Proverbs says:

For as he thinks in his heart, so is he. (Proverbs 23:7)

Take a moment now to be honest with yourself about the way you tend to think when you awake. If you find that your thoughts exhaust rather than energise you, decide to change them for better ones.

But what is the best way to think about the day ahead? Thankfully the Bible says a number of profoundly helpful things about the day we are in. Let's look at some of them.

See today as best spent with God

Today is God's day.

> *This is the day the LORD has made; we will rejoice and be glad in it. (Psalm 118:24)*

If the day belongs to God, then it makes sense to let Him direct it. The Lord calls us to walk with Him through the day. The prophet Micah says:

> *He has shown you, O man, what is good; and what does the Lord require of you but to do justly, to love mercy, and to walk humbly with your God? (Micah 6:8)*

The best way to approach any day is to spend it with God. Determine to walk with Him through the day. Involve Him moment by moment. Share with Him your thoughts and feelings. Talk things through with Him, and make your decisions together. Listen to Him through the day, and follow His guidance in all things.

In order to do this, we first need to come into a personal relationship with Him. Thankfully, Jesus has made this possible by taking our sin upon Himself at the Cross and dying in our place. John says:

> *For God so loved the world that He gave His only begotten Son, that whoever believes in Him should not perish but have everlasting life. (John 3:16)*

If you have not yet taken the step of receiving Christ as your Saviour, and you would like to, pray this prayer:

Lord Jesus, I thank you that you love me, and that you gave your life for me. I admit that I am a sinner, and I confess my sins to you (confess any specific sins to God). I believe that you died and rose again to pay the price for my sin, and to give me the free gift of eternal life. Today I turn from my sin, and ask you to come into my heart as my Saviour and fill me with your Holy Spirit. I receive your gift of eternal life, and I will walk with you forever. Thank you for saving me. Amen.

With Jesus as your Friend, you are now one of the best resourced people in the universe, if you will listen. It is one thing to have a friend, but another thing to spend time with them. Your friendship with Jesus is no exception to this rule. Your Friend seeks you, but you must also seek Him. The wise respond as King David did:

When You said, "Seek My face,' my heart said to You, 'Your face, Lord, I will seek." (Psalm 27:8)

When we seek Him with an open and humble heart, we will find Him and hear His voice. A hard heart will never walk with God. In the warning of Psalm 95:

Today, if you will hear His voice: do not harden your hearts, as in the rebellion, as in the day of trial in the wilderness, when your fathers tested Me; they tried Me, though they saw My work. For forty years I was grieved with that generation, and said, "It is a people who go astray in their hearts, and they do not know My ways." So I swore in My wrath, "They shall not enter My rest." (Psalm 95:7-11)

Hardness of heart must go, pride must go, self righteousness must go. Do not tolerate any such bad attitudes in yourself. Adopt instead an attitude of honesty and humility before God. A right attitude can be adopted in a moment, and will sustain your friendship for a lifetime. Prepare your heart, and bring it to Him as a blank slate on which He, and He alone, may write. He will.

Practice the presence of God as you pass through each day. Imagine that He is with you, and turn to Him often, in the same way that you might turn to a friend physically present with you. Although not generally visible to the physical eye, Christ is truly there, as He promised us in His parting words:

I am with you always, even to the end of the age. (Matthew 28:20)

Talk to the Lord as you walk through the day. Take counsel from Him as you walk together.

See today as a day of blessing

If God is directing your day, you have every reason to rejoice and be glad. Why? Because you are blessed! In the words of an old favourite song of mine:

> *I am blessed, I am blessed,*
> *Every day of my life I am blessed,*
> *When I wake up in the morning,*
> *Or I lay my head to rest,*
> *I am blessed, I am blessed!*

Whatever your circumstances, you need to see each day as a day of blessing. Whether things are going badly or well for you, you are, and you remain, a blessed person. Blessing is an inner reality, before it becomes an outer reality. It is something you are, rather than something you own. It is a state of being, your new nature as a born again child of God. Wherever you go, you carry that blessing. Say to yourself: "I am blessed!"

As you walk with God, today is for you a day of assistance from Heaven. He says:

> *In an acceptable time I have heard you, and in the day of salvation I have helped you.* "Behold, now is the accepted time; behold, now is the day of salvation." (2 Corinthians 6:2)

One way or another, God will help you today. In fact, each new day is one of fresh blessing for you. Like Jeremiah, you need to remind yourself of this, until it becomes an established part of your thinking:

This I recall to my mind, therefore I have hope. Through the LORD'S mercies we are not consumed, because His compassions fail not. They are new every morning; great is Your faithfulness. "The LORD is my portion," says my soul, "Therefore I hope in Him!" The LORD is good to those who wait for Him, to the soul who seeks Him. It is good that one should hope and wait quietly for the salvation of the LORD. (Lamentations 3:21-26).

Spend your day with God and you will enjoy His goodness. Good things happen when we hear what God is saying. Here are some that are specifically listed in the Bible:

You will receive salvation...

Having been born again, not of corruptible seed but incorruptible, through the word of God which lives and abides forever. (1 Peter 1:23)

You will receive faith...

So then faith comes by hearing, and hearing by the word of God. (Romans 10:17)

You will receive freedom...

Then Jesus said to those Jews who believed Him, "If you abide in My word, you are My disciples indeed. And you shall know the truth, and the truth shall make you free. (John 8:31-32)

You will receive insight and understanding...

The entrance of Your words gives light; it gives understanding to the simple. (Psalm 119:130)

You will receive direction and guidance...
Your word is a lamp to my feet and a light to my path. (Psalm 119:105)

You will receive healing...
He sent His word and healed them, and delivered them from their destructions. (Psalm 107:20)

You will receive prosperity...
This Book of the Law shall not depart from your mouth, but you shall meditate in it day and night, that you may observe to do according to all that is written in it. For then you will make your way prosperous, and then you will have good success. (Joshua 1:8)

Listening to God is a daily lifestyle to adopt, rather than a luxury for rare occasions. Diligently practice the presence of God, and you will reach a place where it is natural for you to talk with Him throughout each day, a place where you are more influenced by His word to you than by the circumstances that surround you. This is the place of established faith, described in Psalm 112:

Praise the Lord! Blessed is the man who fears the Lord, who delights greatly in His commandments ... He will not be afraid of evil tidings; his heart is steadfast, trusting in the Lord. His heart is established. He will not be afraid. (Psalm 112:1,7,8)

Never let your circumstances dictate to your faith. All of us will experience changing fortunes as we walk on this earth. It is utter folly to base your view of God on your current level of temporal prosperity or success. Circumstances change, but God is constant. Base your views on His eternal nature and you will stand through the wind and the rain.

You will face enemies that will seek to steal from you, destroy the good in your life, and kill you if they can. At their head is Satan, the arch enemy of the Almighty. One day, Satan will be finally bound and thrown into a lake of fire that burns forever. But for now he is engaged in active warfare against God and humanity. Satan is your number one enemy.

When things go wrong in their lives, some mistakenly blame God. Unless you are opposed to Him, God is not your enemy (and even if you are His enemy, God wants you to be reconciled to Him). God is a good God, who desires good for you. He says:

> *For I know the thoughts that I think toward you, says the Lord, thoughts of peace and not of evil, to give you a future and a hope. Then you will call upon Me and go and pray to Me, and I will listen to you. And you will seek Me and find Me, when you search for Me with all your heart. I will be found by you, says the Lord. (Jeremiah 29:11-14)*

This is the truth. Believe it! Put your trust in the invisible God, rather than in visible things. Don't ignore or deny the circumstances, but neither let them control your mind and overwhelm your faith. *For we walk by faith, not by sight. (2 Corinthians 5:7)*

Seek first the kingdom of God. Face the temporal facts, but always from the vantage point of Heaven. Seek God, listen to Him, and take your stand on the truth of His word to you. Stand here, and stay here, for His word is solid rock, and will always support you. As one hymn writer put it, "All other ground is shifting sand." Whatever the situation, adopt a position of faith, because today, and every day, you are blessed!

2
Prayer for the Day

An Order for Personal Prayer

†

AN ORDER FOR PERSONAL PRAYER AT THE START OF THE DAY

SEEKING GOD
*The Lord is with you. Be still and focus your attention on Him.
Make a mental or written note of whatever He says to you.*

THE LORD'S PRAYER

"Our Father in heaven, hallowed be Your name."
Give thanks and praise to God.

"Your kingdom come.
Your will be done on earth as it is in heaven."
*Pray for yourself and for others that the Lord's will be done
in your lives today. Ask the Lord to show you what He wants
you to do today, and wait for His reply.*

"Give us this day our daily bread."
Bring specific needs to God, and trust in Him.

"And forgive us our debts, as we forgive our debtors."
*Ask the Spirit to show you your sins. Repent of them all.
Forgive all those who have wronged you in any way.*

"And do not lead us into temptation, but deliver us from the evil one."
*Resist the devil. With full authority in Christ, command him,
"Go, in Jesus' name!" from your life, and from the lives
of those for whom you pray.*

"For Yours is the kingdom and the power and the glory forever. Amen."

BIBLE READING & MEDITATION
*Read the Bible passages and meditation for the day, applying them to
yourself and to your life.*

Seeking God

Of all the activities that you could pursue today, there is one that takes precedence over all others. In the New Testament story of Mary and Martha, we find Jesus underlining the primacy of this one act:

> *Now it happened as they went that He entered a certain village; and a certain woman named Martha welcomed Him into her house. And she had a sister called Mary, who also sat at Jesus' feet and heard His word. But Martha was distracted with much serving, and she approached Him and said, "Lord, do You not care that my sister has left me to serve alone? Therefore tell her to help me." And Jesus answered and said to her, "Martha, Martha, you are worried and troubled about many things. But one thing is needed, and Mary has chosen that good part, which will not be taken away from her." (Luke 10:38-42)*

There is nothing more valuable that you can do today than to seek God. Christ invites you to sit at His feet and listen. He makes it clear that this is the one thing you need to do in order to live a truly successful life. Then He waits to see whether you will follow His guidance, or waste your life on other things. If you make seeking God your daily priority, everything else will fall into place. Make it the foundation of your day.

How do you seek God? If you are new to this kind of meditation, follow these guidelines to get started. At the beginning, you may find it helpful to find a quiet place and a comfortable chair. A quiet setting will help you concentrate and focus your mind. With practice, you will be able to seek

God in busy and noisy settings, but at the start this may be difficult. If you cannot find a quiet place, it is still perfectly possible to develop the skill of seeking God. It is just a bit easier to start in a quiet place.

Begin by relaxing and being physically still. Put from your mind any thoughts that clamour for your attention. Write down anything important that you are afraid of forgetting.

Next, imagine that God is with you. You may find it helpful to picture Jesus by your side. God is omnipresent. In other words, He is everywhere. He is with you now, and His desire is to talk with you.

As you focus your attention on Him, imagine that He says something to you. This is not as crazy as it might sound. God is really there, and you are using your imagination to connect with Him. Because God is invisible, you must use your imagination to communicate.

Jesus said, *"My sheep hear My voice, and I know them, and they follow Me"* (John 10:27). What do you hear Him say? Make a mental or written note of it. Then turn your attention back to Him and listen again. What more does He say? Again, make a note. Continue in this way, until you sense that you have finished.

Practice seeking God daily and you will soon come to recognise His voice. You will also learn to distinguish His voice from other voices. The writer of Hebrews talks of, *"Those who by reason of use have their senses exercised to discern both good and evil"* (Hebrews 5:14). As you use your spiritual senses in this way, your ability to discriminate between voices will grow, and you will reach a place where you are able to consistently identify each one.

Learning to discriminate between voices is important because God's voice is not the only one we may hear. There are others, including your own inner voice. We all talk to ourselves within the privacy of our mind. We may also be spoken to by demonic forces, tempting us to sin, some of which try to trick us by impersonating God's voice. By seeking God daily, we develop the ability to discern both good and evil.

Always check out what you hear, in order to ensure, as far as you can, that you are hearing from Heaven. When God is speaking, you will have an inner witness in your heart, for His word is truth. Test everything against the Spirit and the word. Be particularly careful in the early stages of learning to listen to God, when your ability to reliably identify demonic sources has not yet fully developed.

Because of the possibility of deception, some reject the practice of seeking God. This is not only a grave error, but a great sin. God has called us to seek Him. The answer to deception is not to stop seeking, but to develop discernment. Diligently practice listening to God and you will develop the discernment that you need.

From the beginning, God will speak to you. Jesus said:

> *So I say to you, ask, and it will be given to you; seek, and you will find; knock, and it will be opened to you. For everyone who asks receives, and he who seeks finds, and to him who knocks it will be opened. If a son asks for bread from any father among you, will he give him a stone? Or if he asks for a fish, will he give him a serpent instead of a fish? Or if he asks for an egg, will he offer him a scorpion? If you then, being evil, know how to give good gifts to your children, how much more will your heavenly Father give the Holy Spirit to those who ask Him? (Luke 11:9-13)*

However busy you may be, never neglect this primary spiritual discipline, but seek God at the start of each new day, and as often as you can.

The Lord's Prayer

When the disciples came to Jesus and asked Him how they should pray, He said:

> *When you pray, you shall not be like the hypocrites. For they love to pray standing in the synagogues and on the corners of the streets, that they may be seen by men. Assuredly, I say to you, they have their reward. But you, when you pray, go into your room, and when you have shut your door, pray to your Father who is in the secret place; and your Father who sees in secret will reward you openly. And when you pray, do not use vain repetitions as the heathen do. For they think that they will be heard for their many words. Therefore do not be like them. For your Father knows the things you have need of before you ask Him. In this manner, therefore, pray:*
>
> *Our Father in heaven,*
> *Hallowed be Your name.*
> *Your kingdom come.*
> *Your will be done,*
> *On earth as it is in Heaven.*
> *Give us this day our daily bread.*
> *And forgive us our debts,*
> *As we forgive our debtors.*
> *And do not lead us into temptation,*
> *But deliver us from the evil one.*
> *For Yours is the kingdom and the power and the glory forever.*
> *Amen.*
>
> (Matthew 6:5-13)

This prayer that Jesus taught us contains all that we need to cover in our personal prayer times, and provides the most excellent framework for our intercession.

"Our Father in heaven, hallowed be Your name"

It is right to give thanks and praise to God. This is a good place to start. The psalmist says:

> *Enter into His gates with thanksgiving, and into His courts with praise. Be thankful to Him, and bless His name. For the Lord is good; His mercy is everlasting, and His truth endures to all generations. (Psalm 100:4,5)*

On one occasion when the disciples were celebrating the power of Jesus' name over the demonic world, Jesus said to them, *"Do not rejoice in this, that the spirits are subject to you, but rather rejoice that your names are written in Heaven"* (Luke 10:20). Whatever great things God has done for us, or through us, one thing alone stands out as worthy of the highest praise and most heartfelt thanks: the fact that He has saved us. Above all, thank God that your name is written in the Lamb's Book of Life (Revelation 21:27).

"Your kingdom come, Your will be done on earth as it is in heaven"

Pray for yourself and for others that the Lord's will be done in your lives today. You may wish to name those for whom you pray, committing them to God's care, and praying that His will prevails in each one's life.

In relation to yourself, ask the Lord to show you what He would have you do today, and wait for His reply. There may be one or two things that He shows you as being particularly important. Make these a priority. You may find it helpful to make a note of them, perhaps entering them in your diary, in order to help ensure that you do not forget.

"Give us this day our daily bread"

There may be specific needs that you, or others known to you, are currently facing. Bring them to God, believing that He will resolve every one. Listen to whatever He may say to you about each one.

"And forgive us our debts, as we forgive our debtors"

Ask the Holy Spirit to show you your sins, and repent of them all. True repentance is a change of heart and mind that leads to a change of behaviour.

Forgive all those who have wronged you in any way. Remember the words of Jesus, who said:

> *If you forgive men their trespasses, your heavenly Father will also forgive you. But if you do not forgive men their trespasses, neither will your Father forgive your trespasses. (Matthew 6:14,15)*

"And do not lead us into temptation, but deliver us from the evil one"

A spiritual battle is being fought out on earth, and we live in the midst of it. You have an enemy, and you need to know how to defeat him. Peter writes:

> *Be sober, be vigilant; because your adversary the devil walks about like a roaring lion, seeking whom he may devour. Resist him, steadfast in the faith. (1 Peter 5:8,9)*

How do you defeat the evil one? Peter and James give the same advice: *"Submit to God. Resist the devil and he will flee from you" (James 4:7).* From a place of humble submission to God, take your stand against the devil, and resist him. With full authority in Christ, command him, "Go, in Jesus' name!" from your life, and from the lives of those for whom you pray.

"For Yours is the kingdom and the power and the glory forever, Amen"

This unique prayer ends as it began, with praise and thanks to God.

Bible reading and meditation

Neither your day, nor your life, will be complete without Scripture! Paul says to Timothy:

> *From childhood you have known the Holy Scriptures, which are able to make you wise for salvation through faith which is in Christ Jesus. All Scripture is given by inspiration of God, and is profitable for doctrine, for reproof, for correction, for instruction in righteousness, that the man of God may be complete, thoroughly equipped for every good work.*
> *(2 Timothy 3:15-17)*

Part Three of this book contains a programme for reading through the whole Bible in one year. With each daily meditation you will find the Scripture readings for the day. These consist of two or three Bible chapters.

Before you read, ask the Holy Spirit who inspired the Scriptures, to open the eyes of your understanding to the truth contained within them.

As you read the Bible, develop the habit of applying its truth to your own life. By this means you will derive the maximum benefit from your reading. Judge yourself in the light of truth, and change your thoughts and actions wherever necessary. It only takes a moment to change your position.

The meditations in Part Three are written to encourage and inspire you in your daily walk with God. Like the recommended Scripture readings, they are undated, so that they may be used in any or every year. Some are directly linked to the Scripture readings. All seek to convey the principles of truly abundant living.

3
The Meditations

JANUARY

January 1 *Genesis 1, 2 Chronicles 1, Daniel 1*

Make history this year

What a privilege it is, to be living in the years following the life, death and ascension of our Lord and Saviour Jesus Christ. For many centuries they looked forward to the coming of Christ the Messiah, and to the outpouring of the Holy Spirit on all. Many desired to see the events that are now history to us. That history is still being made today. As we stand in the first day of a new year, we can choose to make our own personal contribution to the book of Acts, the New Testament book that is still being written. That contribution starts with seeking the Lord. Do what God sent you to do, and Heaven will record that you changed history for the better this year!

January 2 *Genesis 2, 2 Chronicles 2, Daniel 2*

Be a builder and a maintainer

The capacity for creativity and care is part of what it means to be made in God's image (Genesis 1:26-28). The Creator and Sustainer placed in us the same kind of nature. Are you in touch with your creative self, the part of you that builds and develops? And do you recognise your caring self, the dimension of your being that maintains and preserves? We need to express these attributes under the inspiration of the Holy Spirit, building and maintaining as directed by Him. As the actors on earth's stage, let us look to the Director each day and do our best, not only to enjoy maintaining what is good, but also to extend our reach, going beyond and building more, for the love of God and the benefit of others.

January 3 *Genesis 3, 2 Chronicles 3, Daniel 3*

Don't hide from God

God's first recorded question in the Bible is, *"Where are you?" (Genesis 3:9)*. Adam and Eve had just eaten the forbidden fruit, and the effect was devastating. One moment they had been freely enjoying the utopia of Eden, the next they were so gripped by fear that they hid. Hiding was a waste of time, and they knew it. No one can hide from God. But their fear was so intense that they were desperate. It has been said that everyone is hiding something. How about you? What are you hiding? Whatever it is, there is no need to hide it from God. Christ has paid the price of sin in full. Confess your sin, come out of hiding today, and enjoy the freedom that only God's love and acceptance of you can bring.

January 4 *Genesis 4, 2 Chronicles 4, Daniel 4*

Rule over sin

The world's first murder was about to be committed. Cain was very angry, so God said to him, *"If you do well, will you not be accepted? And if you do not well, sin lies at the door. And its desire is for you, but you should rule over it" (Genesis 4:7)*. His goal was to be accepted by God despite his unacceptable offering. When God rejected his offering, Cain was angry. Instead of taking God's advice and changing, Cain nursed his grievance and killed his brother Abel, whose offering God had accepted. Cain not only failed to rule over sin, but became its servant and did its will. Don't feed your anger – it will only get worse. Starve it by turning to God and doing what He says. Make it your aim to please Him.

January 5 *Genesis 5, 2 Chronicles 5, Daniel 5*

Be anxious for nothing!

Everyone experiences anxiety to some degree. Anxiety is generated whenever we are uncertain about things that are important to us. When you are anxious, take your fears to God in prayer. Share your heart with Him, and keep praying until you have prayed it through. As you do, listen to God, and take note of anything He says to you. When you have prayed it through and received whatever you need to get from God, you will feel a peace inside. This is, *"The peace of God, which surpasses all understanding" (Philippians 4:7)*. It will guard your heart and mind. Keep going back to God, whenever you feel anxious, and stay in the peace of God. Be anxious for nothing!

January 6 *Genesis 6, 2 Chronicles 6, Daniel 6*

Go from fear to faith

Many people, when they wake, start the day by considering their problems rather than by counting their blessings. This leads inevitably to a state of anxiety or discontent and, if practised over a long enough period it can become an established attitude or mind-set that is difficult to break. There is a different path that leads to contentment and joy, rather than undue stress and anxiety. It is the path of gratitude. The apostle Paul was able to write, *"I have learned in whatever state I am, to be content" (Philippians 4:11)*. Each morning, thank God for all His blessings to you. Use your mind to imagine solutions rather than problems, and make the journey from fear to faith!

January 7 *Genesis 7, 2 Chronicles 7, Daniel 7*

Immerse yourself in God

Isaiah says to ancient Israel, *"Oh, that you had heeded My commandments! Then your peace would have been like a river, and your righteousness like the waves of the sea" (Isaiah 48:18).* Heed what God is saying to you, and powerful forces of peace and righteousness will be loosed in your soul. Look at the waves of the sea. Imagine them rolling in again and again, crashing against the shore with great clouds of spray. God's love is like that, ever flowing to you, with no limit, no end. As you seek Him and heed His word, the breakers of His love will wash over you, cleansing, healing, strengthening, and guiding. He will refresh and invigorate your whole being as you immerse yourself in Him. What is God saying to you today?

January 8 *Genesis 8, 2 Chronicles 8, Daniel 8*

Wait for the tide

God has set creation to function in a manner that tends to be wavy rather than flat, variable rather than linear. He says, *"While the earth remains, seedtime and harvest, cold and heat, winter and summer, and day and night shall not cease" (Genesis 8:22).* There is a flow to it. Like the tide, life has its 'ins and outs', its 'ups and downs'. That is why the writer of Ecclesiastes says to, *"Cast your bread upon the waters, for you will find it after many days" (Ecclesiastes 11:1).* It is as though what we give will be taken by the tide, and then brought back to us later by the same waters, perhaps at a time when we desperately need it. What you give you will never lose. So go with the flow. Wait and catch the tide.

January 9 *Genesis 9, 2 Chronicles 9, Daniel 9*

Spend time in the Spirit

'In the Spirit' is the place to be. When you are in this place, you may receive great things from God. When in the spirit, the apostle John received the amazing visions that make up the final book of the Bible. Peter was in this state when God showed him that He wanted the gospel to go to non-Jews (Acts 10:9-16). This place was Paul's determined focus, the foundation of his miracle ministry at Corinth and in all the churches (1 Corinthians 2:2-5). Daniel was in this place when the angel Gabriel showed him the future (Daniel 9:20,21). What will God show you as you spend time in this place? Follow your passion for God. Get caught up in prayer and praise whenever you can. Don't miss out – get in the Spirit!

January 10 *Genesis 10, 2 Chronicles 10, Daniel 10*

Don't try to do God's job for Him

Various things can discourage us from praying for healing. Some people do not pray, because they doubt whether healing will take place. They may fear that if they pray for others and nothing happens, they will look foolish, or be seen as a charlatan. Others decide to wait until God gives them the power to heal, before they start praying for the sick. Sadly, in many cases they will wait forever, not because they lack power, but because they misunderstand the nature of the task. Your job is not to heal. Healing is God's prerogative. You cannot heal anyone. Your job is to pray in faith. That is something you *can* do. It is well within your power. Do not try to do God's job for him! Simply play your part.

January 11   *Genesis 11, 2 Chronicles 11, Daniel 11*

Smash the idol of work

How important is work to you? For some, work becomes an idol, something they love more than God. Even Christian ministry becomes idolatrous if it takes the central place reserved for Christ in your heart. Don't put working *for* God in the place of walking *with* God. The work you do on earth is important, but you must remember that the work of God flows out of the love of God. To do the greatest work, you must walk the greatest walk. God has planned your work from eternity and He is the only one who can direct it. So examine yourself each day, to check that God alone holds the highest place in your heart and that you are following His directions. The greatest work flows from the highest place.

January 12   *Genesis 12, 2 Chronicles 12, Daniel 12*

Love actively

Love changes things, but only when it is both an attitude and an action. As an attitude, love permeates our inner world, predisposing us to act in compassionate ways, so that we are more likely to respond lovingly. As an action, love transforms our outer world, and lives are touched by God. Let us practice love until it becomes our automatic response. The best way to develop any habit is to practice it. Why not start now? Try this simple exercise. Write a list of some, or all, of the people you will meet today. Note down their names and alongside each write one loving thing you will do for that person today. At the end of the day, review the list and thank God for the good that has been done. Don't be passive - love actively!

January 13 *Genesis 13, 2 Chronicles 13, Hosea 1*

Pray in faith

What does it mean to pray in faith? The writer of Hebrews tells us that, *"Faith is the substance of things hoped for, the evidence of things not seen" (Hebrews 11:1).* Faith is that trust or conviction we experience as a direct consequence of hearing God. It is the substance and the evidence of our hope. Without faith, hope is vaporous, but with it, hope takes physical form as the hungry are fed, the sick are healed, and the oppressed are set free. Whenever you pray, listen to God, and your faith will grow in line with whatever He says. You will then have no problem praying with conviction. Do not try to convince yourself or to fabricate faith. Know your Bible, pray what God tells you to pray, and you will pray in faith.

January 14 *Genesis 14, 2 Chronicles 14, Hosea 2*

Learn from your anger

There is a message in anger that you need to hear, and that message is the reason for your anger. When we are angry, we should ask ourselves the question that God asked Cain: *"Why are you angry?" (Genesis 4:6).* Be honest with yourself and be honest with God about your anger, and the thinking that is causing it. If your anger is the result of wrong thinking, ask God to give you His perspective. Then change your mind, bringing your viewpoint into line with His. If your anger comes from right thinking, ask God to show you how to respond. Then do what He says, working for righteousness, justice, and truth. Learn to read the message that anger contains, and take that message to God.

January 15 *Genesis 15, 2 Chronicles 15, Hosea 3*

Remember your blessings

Look at the sky. That is what God told Abraham to do. *"He brought him outside and said, 'Look now toward the heavens and count the stars, if you are able to count them.' And He said to him, 'So shall your seed be'" (Genesis 15:5).* This is how God impressed on him the number of his descendents. Abraham did not live to see all those descendents. He had to trust God that it would be so. But God fulfilled His promise. You too are blessed more than you know. Paul says that, *"'Eye has not seen, nor ear heard,' nor has it entered into the heart of man, 'the things which God has prepared for those who love Him'" (1 Corinthians 2:9).* Your calling is not Abraham's, but thanks to Christ's sacrifice you are just as blessed! (Galatians 3:14).

January 16 *Genesis 16, 2 Chronicles 16, Hosea 4*

Tell God your secret fears

You may have fears that you do not share with others, but you need not carry them alone. God knows all your anxieties, worries, and concerns. He already knows your deepest fears, so there is no need to keep quiet about them in His presence, and everything to be gained by discussing them with Him. When you are next troubled, share it with God. Talk together about it. Allow Him to calm your troubled heart, for His word brings peace. As you hear His word on it, your peace will be restored. Do not try to carry these fears alone. There is no need. Come and talk to Him about each one, and deal with them together. As you share your heart with Him, He will share His heart with you, and your peace will return.

January 17 *Genesis 17, 2 Chronicles 17, Hosea 5*

Treat yourself well

When we think about relationships we do not always consider the person we will be talking to from the cradle to the grave, and beyond. I am talking about your relationship with yourself. It is not unusual for people to invest far more in relationships with others than they invest in the self-relationship. And yet the self relationship is foundational to all other human relationships. If we are unpleasant to ourselves, how are we going to treat others? What is your relationship like with yourself? Listen in to your own inner dialogue. If someone else spoke to you the way you speak to yourself, what would you think? If you are not happy with what you hear, go to work today and treat yourself well.

January 18 *Genesis 18, 2 Chronicles 18, Hosea 6*

Face your obstacles

At times we must face challenges and difficulties in order to get to where God is leading us. There are obstacles to be overcome along the way, and some may be very great indeed. For Israel, there was the seemingly impenetrable barrier of the Red Sea standing between them and the Promised Land. For Christ and the disciples, there was a life threatening storm blocking their mission to save a demonised man. For Saint Paul, there were the determined attempts of his enemies to kill him before his mission even got going. What will you have to face, to do what God has called you to do? Whatever it is, do not fear, for on this path you will surely overcome. Trust God today that you *will* make it.

January 19   *Genesis 19, 2 Chronicles 19, Hosea 7*

Look back with God

What do you see when you look over your shoulder? We all look back from time to time, but the way we do it can either help or harm us. There is a way to look back that can turn disasters into successes and defeats into victories, but we do not always take it. Lot's wife looked back when she should have pressed on, and was turned into a pillar of salt (Genesis 19:26). The right way is to look back with God, as He directs. When we look back with thanksgiving for all He has brought us through, we are strengthened at the very core of our being. Look back with Him, and He will heal the pain of your past. Include Him in your reminiscences, hear His thoughts on each one, and somehow He will turn it to your good.

January 20   *Genesis 20, 2 Chronicles 20, Hosea 8*

Plan your diary with God

Time management skills may help you to organise your life effectively, but they cannot ensure that your works will be the right ones. Effective time management without God's guidance merely creates well organised and efficient sinners. Do not plan your diary until you have sought the Lord. It is better by far to do one small work that God requested, than to be showered with earthly honours for 'great works' He did not order. The direction we receive in prayer at the start of the day should be the action we perform in the remainder of the day. Manage your time like this, and you will one day hear those wonderful words, *"Well done, good and faithful servant" (Matthew 25:21).*

January 21   *Genesis 21, 2 Chronicles 21, Hosea 9*

Deal with rogue thoughts

As you identify, understand, and reject untrue or unhelpful thoughts, you may find that some are harder to remove than others. This may be because they have been practised and reinforced repeatedly over a long period. Such thoughts may return persistently, and it may seem as though they will never cease. When this happens, do not give up. Although more resistant to extinction, even these persistent thoughts will yield to you in the end. They must do, because you are in charge. Remember that your calm continued rejection of unwanted thoughts will result in their eventual disappearance. However many times they return, answer them with the truth, and their power will be destroyed.

January 22   *Genesis 22, 2 Chronicles 22, Hosea 10*

Reject doubt and unbelief

Where truth is relative, as in the formulations of science or the deductions of the private detective, doubt is of great value, prompting the investigator to question their current theory and seek a more accurate understanding. But where truth is absolute, as in the word of God, doubt is not only worthless, but a great enemy. When Peter doubted Jesus' word, he began to sink, despite having successfully walked on water! Christ says to him, *"O you of little faith! Why did you doubt?"* (Matthew 14:31). When we pray, we should reject all doubt concerning what God has said. Keep your spiritual senses fixed on God as you pray. By so doing, you will keep your faith strong, and be ready to repel all doubt.

January 23   *Genesis 23, 2 Chronicles 23, Hosea 11*

Focus on God Himself

There are times in spiritual development when our excitement over our present life in the Spirit may decline. For example, when people are first baptised in the Holy Spirit, they often enjoy the exhilaration of speaking in tongues. After a while the effervescence fades, and they may wonder what is happening to them and why. The answer is a positive one. God is drawing us to Himself. He wants to move our focus away from the *manifestation* of God, and to get our heart and mind focused on HIMSELF! The goal of true spiritual development is not the manifestation of miracles, signs and wonders, marvellous though they may be, but nothing less than union with God Himself. Focus on God, your Source.

January 24   *Genesis 24, 2 Chronicles 24, Hosea 12*

Thank God for your unique identity

As far as science can tell, there is only one physical universe. But there are billions of inner worlds. Each human life represents a different personal universe, possessing a distinct identity. Your Self is different to my Self. Each of us has a set of personal characteristics, physical and non-physical, that make us unique. Throughout history there has never been anyone like you. Neither will there ever be anyone like you. There are those who may look like you, or are similar to you in other respects, but there is no one identical to you in every way. As a great work, and the only one of its kind in existence, you are of very great value indeed. Thank God for your unique identity.

January 25 Genesis 25, 2 Chronicles 25, Hosea 13

Say the right thing

Listen carefully to yourself as you speak to others, and you may be surprised. Imagine what it might be like for them, to be spoken to like that. Our words, tone of voice, and body language, all combine to send a message. Listen honestly to that message, and identify it. Is this a good message to send? Is this the message you *really* should send? The greatest test of any message is to ask whether it is a true and timely expression of God's love. Divine love can inspire all our words and actions, if we will let it. Test your messages today, and see how they rate. The key is to listen and learn. With practice, your words, tone, and body language will increasingly convey the right message.

January 26 Genesis 26, 2 Chronicles 26, Hosea 14

Make God your refuge

Knowing that we need it, God has provided the greatest protection of all: Himself! It is as though He says, *"I'll be your security."* Solomon says, *"The name of the Lord is a strong tower; the righteous run to it and are safe"* (Proverbs 18:10). David says, *"The Lord is my rock and my fortress and my deliverer; my God, my strength, in whom I will trust; my shield and the strength of my salvation, my stronghold"* (Psalm 18:2). The strength we need is found in God alone. The key to acquiring this defence and to abandoning our unhelpful defences is to make God our refuge. As we daily turn to Him, the light of the Spirit fills our heart, and each redundant defence is exposed and removed. There is no safer place than the fortress of the Lord.

January 27 *Genesis 27, 2 Chronicles 27, Joel 1*

Thank God for the Bible

The hand of God is visible all around us. From the smallest cells to the tallest mountains, we can see His awesome handiwork. But although creation provides clear evidence of a Creator, its message is open to interpretation. For example, two people can view the same sunset and see different expressions of God. The Bible, in contrast, gives us a clear message, for in it God has spoken in propositional form. We have clear statements about things, as well as stories that illustrate those truths in the lives of biblical characters. Thank God for the Bible. Thank God that He has made certain things clear. He has not told us everything we would *like* to know, but He has told us everything we *need* to know.

January 28 *Genesis 28, 2 Chronicles 28, Joel 2*

Love God not money

Financial prosperity can be a great blessing, but only if we handle it properly. A common mistake is to depend on money more than on God. When wealth abounds, it is easy to trust in it, for material and financial riches cushion those who possess them against many hardships and difficulties of life. But money is not God. It has been said that it makes a good servant, but a bad master. Wealth can be used for great good, but the moment we develop an inordinate desire for it, we fall. Saint Paul says, *"The love of money is a root of all evils, of which some having lusted after, they were seduced from the faith and pierced themselves through with many sorrows"* (1 Timothy 6:10). Guard your heart and keep God as your Source.

January 29   *Genesis 29, 2 Chronicles 29, Joel 3*

Keep a positive focus

When taking a photo, a photographer selects a subject, and then adjusts the camera lens to bring the subject into sharp focus. We too should be careful when we select a topic for our mind to focus on. The focus we choose will profoundly influence both our own lives, and the lives of others. For example, it is possible to develop a negative focus, so that we become consistently down or depressed, or to acquire an anxious focus, so that we continually worry about things. St Paul encourages us to maintain a positive focus. He says, *"Whatever things are true ... noble ... just ... pure ... lovely ... of good report – meditate on these things" (Philippians 4:8)*. Choose your subject, and focus your mind today.

January 30   *Genesis 30, 2 Chronicles 30, Amos 1*

Learn from your failures

It has been said that failure often contains the seed of later success. We can learn from failure, if we choose to. As every inventor and true pioneer knows, failure has a lesson to teach us. Each time Thomas Edison failed in his attempts to make an electric light, he discovered yet another way *not* to make a light bulb. After thousands of such failures, or should we say learning opportunities, electric light was born. We are blessed with such light because Edison learnt from failure. What great blessings await us, if we too will learn from failure? If your cause is right, do not give up when you fail, but go to God, and let Him teach you the lesson to be learnt. Apply those lessons, and your failures will be turned to successes.

January 31 *Genesis 31, 2 Chronicles 31, Amos 2*

Know your value to God

How valuable do you think you are? The Cross is the most powerful and eloquent statement of human value that has ever, or will ever, be made. For it was at the Cross that Jesus Christ took our place, carried our sins, and received the punishment we deserved. He was our substitute. For the exchange to work, the sacrifice had to be of *equal value* to those for whom it was made. So God sent His Son. Because of this, you may safely conclude that when the Father looks at you, He sees you as being as valuable as Jesus! If this truth were to fully grip your soul, you would never have a self-worth problem! Say, *"I'm as valuable as Jesus!"* until you believe and never doubt it.

February

February 1   *Genesis 32, 2 Chronicles 32, Amos 3*

Stay humble

It is right to strive for success in the things that God has called us to, but we should be aware that success often brings its own challenges. Where success means that we are blessed with wealth and power, there will also be many temptations. Pride is a particular danger. At one point in his reign King Hezekiah fell into this trap. We read that, *"His heart was lifted up; therefore wrath was looming over him"* (2 Chronicles 32:25). Thankfully, disaster was avoided, for, *"Hezekiah humbled himself for the pride of his heart"* (v.26). The wise put humility at the heart of their success strategies. Stay small in your own eyes, trust God, and do what He tells you. That is the way to face the challenges of both success and failure.

February 2   *Genesis 33, 2 Chronicles 33, Amos 4*

Be the best

God has prepared a great and unique work for you to do, whilst you are on earth. As you take this path and follow it, without turning aside from any of the words which He commands you, you will be the best, the very best, at what you do. In Heaven's sight there is no higher position on earth that you can ever hold than the role God has called you to. Choose another path, however exalted by men, and you will only ever be second rate in God's evaluation. Earth may applaud you for a season, but Heaven will never be deceived. In eternity, many of the first will be last, and many of the last will be first. Choose Heaven's path of humility and obedience to God, the path of true greatness. Be the best.

February 3   *Genesis 34, 2 Chronicles 34, Amos 5*

Prosper by Heaven's values

How would you describe your values? Earth and Heaven have very different value systems. This world honours wealth, achievement, and power, but in the sight of Heaven, whatever we do for God, even if it is only to give someone a cup of water, has eternal value, and will be rewarded by Him (Matthew 10:42). It is only when we evaluate our life in the light of Heaven's values that we get an accurate assessment of our work. Take a moment now to measure your activity against the yardstick of Heaven. How much is inspired by Heaven's values, and how much by Earth's? Maximise the value of your work today by choosing to work according to Heaven's values! Do what matters to God. He will show you.

February 4   *Genesis 35, 2 Chronicles 35, Amos 6*

Pray before you pray

Throughout the gospels we read of how people brought the sick to Christ that He might lay hands on them and heal them (cf. Matthew 4:24; Mark 1:32; Luke 4:40). We do a similar thing now when we pray for the sick. We cannot take them physically to Jesus, but we can bring them to Him in prayer. If we believe that God is the Healer, we will go to Him whenever there is a need for healing. Before you pray for someone to be healed, look to God and listen to Him. He will guide you, showing you whatever you need to know in order to pray effectively. When you pray for the sick, stop and listen to Him, if only for a moment. Let Him guide you, and your prayers will be backed by Heaven. Pray before you pray.

February 5   *Genesis 36, 2 Chronicles 36, Amos 7*

Start and stop with God

How do you deal with stress? People commonly respond in one of two ways when faced with stressful situations: they will either fight the problem, or flee from it. It takes wisdom to know when to push on, and when to pull back. Let God give you that wisdom. If you walk with Him diligently, and listen carefully, He will show you when to go, and when to stop. The best way to deal with stress is the way God directs. As you receive His directions, they will build faith in your heart, and you will receive the strength to do *whatever* is required. Remember that you walk by faith, and not by sight. When you are under stress, be moved by what you believe, rather than by what you see. Take God's directions today.

February 6   *Genesis 37, Ezra 1, Amos 8*

Knock on God's doors

Jesus taught the importance of taking action. He said, *"Ask, and it will be given to you; seek, and you will find; knock, and it will be opened to you" (Matthew 7:7).* Once we have heard from Heaven it is imperative that we act. Many a dream dies for lack of action. However difficult the mission, if we will step out, God will make a way! He will open doors for us, but *we* must push forwards. Knock and the door *will* be opened. You have a part to play. Take your directions from Heaven, and then act. Do it, however impossible it seems, and He will open *all* the doors required. Satan also opens doors, so be discriminating. Don't look at the doors, but look to God. He will show you the right way. Take the next step today.

February 7 *Genesis 38, Ezra 2, Amos 9*

Navigate by the light of eternity

John introduces us to Christ as the Light that shines in the darkness (John 1:5). Come to Him, and you come to the light. He is like the sun, shining in all its brilliance. Lift up your eyes and see. Lift your eyes to Heaven, where Christ is seated at the right hand of God. His light will surely guide you. Just as mariners navigate by the stars, so you must navigate by the light of eternity. Chart your course by Heaven's light, and God will bless your voyage. Your ship will not founder on the rocks, but your mission *will* be successful. Though you face many storms, you will weather them all, for Jesus is with you in the boat. You *will* make it, for no earthly storm clouds, however dark, can block this Light. Navigate by it always.

February 8 *Genesis 39, Ezra 3, Obadiah 1*

Check it out

Jesus spoke about the need to see others clearly. Communication involves guessing what the other person thinks, and then checking to see whether we have got it right. Many problems are caused by our failure to properly check out our hunches. We assume that others think and feel in certain ways, but we may be utterly wrong. The actions we take, based on such false assumptions, are bound to be inappropriate, and can lead to negative outcomes. To avoid this danger, we should ask the other person to tell us whether we have correctly understood them. This will enable us to modify our view, and bring it into line with the truth. Test your assumptions, and enjoy better relationships today.

February 9 *Genesis 40, Ezra 4, Jonah 1*

Be diligent

A fool perseveres when God says to stop, but the wise persevere in the face of adversity. Both your calling and your character require diligence in order to blossom fully. Saint Peter says, *"Giving all diligence, add to your faith virtue, to virtue knowledge, to knowledge self-control, to self-control perseverance, to perseverance godliness, to godliness brotherly kindness, and to brotherly kindness love"* (2 Peter 1:5-7). Are we to build all these attributes by our own efforts alone? By no means! If you give all diligence to seeking God and obeying Him, He will develop your character and your calling. The key is cooperation. In the words of the hymn writer, *"Trust and obey, for there's no other way."* Be diligent to follow Him today.

February 10 *Genesis 41, Ezra 5, Jonah 2*

Give and grow

When Joseph interpreted Pharaoh's dreams, he revealed a key principle of resource management (Genesis 41:1-37). Build up stocks in times of plenty, and you will be better prepared for lean times. Save in the day of prosperity that you may spend in the day of poverty. Some spend without restraint, others save all they can, but the wise balance spending, saving, and giving. For many, giving plays no part in their personal or business management. Yet giving is a fundamental principle of economic growth. Jesus said, *"Give and it will be given to you: good measure, pressed down, shaken together, and running over will be put into your bosom. For with the same measure that you use, it will be measured back to you"* (Luke 6:38).

February 11   *Genesis 42, Ezra 6, Jonah 3*

Choose your destiny

Every life ever lived on earth reflects the same pattern, a series of events ordained by God in Heaven. God creates a human spirit (Zechariah 12:1), gives it power to choose what it will become (John 1:12), and receives it back on death (Ecclesiastes 12:7). Finally, it is judged and assigned an appropriate place in eternity (Revelation 20:11-15). God has given every human being the power to determine what they will become, and where they will spend eternity. Every choice shapes both your development and your future. So choose life! Spend your days with God, and embrace your divine destiny. One thing is needful – to sit at the feet of Jesus, to listen and to obey (John 10:38-42).

February 12   *Genesis 43, Ezra 7, Jonah 4*

Keep your eyes on Jesus

Speaking of events that would occur before His return, Jesus said, *"And when these things begin to happen, then look up and lift up your heads, for your redemption draws near" (Luke 21:28).* This list of signs contains some chilling developments, events that cause great distress and suffering. That is why He says, *"Look up!"* The tribulation is finite and will pass, but it heralds Christ's eternal reign. Jesus is coming back in victory. Angels announced: *"This same Jesus who is taken up from you into Heaven, will come in the way you have seen Him going into Heaven" (Acts 1:11).* John says, *"Behold, He comes with the clouds, and every eye will see Him" (Revelation 1:7).* We have something good to look forwards to, a sure hope. Look up!

February 13 *Genesis 44, Ezra 8, Micah 1*

Catch the wind

Some quench the Holy Spirit, but they can never contain Him. Like the wind, He moves freely, wherever He will. Try to control the Holy Spirit, and you will lose Him. Being unlimited and eternal, He cannot be contained. When He gives us His Spirit, God gives us the uncontainable. The Spirit flows from our heart as, *"Rivers of living water" (John 7:38)*. He is infinitely flexible in His action to achieve God's purposes. Like water He always finds a course. So do not try to control the Spirit, for if you resist Him, He will withdraw from you. Rather let Him lead you. Sense His flow, and trust yourself to it. The Holy Spirit knows the way. Follow Him, and you will complete the work that God has given you to do.

February 14 *Genesis 45, Ezra 9, Micah 2*

Keep hold of the wheel

Just as a driver must keep hold of the wheel, so you need to remain in control of your life, under God. It is vital that you keep hold of the wheel. There may be those who would like to take that wheel, in order to fulfil some agenda of their own. Resist them in the Lord. It is absolutely imperative for the purposes of the Kingdom, that you do not relinquish executive control of the ministry that God has given you. You and you alone, have been given the responsibility and privilege of doing that work. Listen to others, treat them well, and work with them where you can, but never abdicate your role. Don't follow other people – follow God! Keep your hands on the wheel, and take His way, everyday.

February 15   *Genesis 46, Ezra 10, Micah 3*

Manage your mind

How do you manage your mind? God gave us the capacity to think, but how we use that capacity is up to us. Unmanaged, our thoughts may be disorganised, or even dysfunctional. Good mental management starts with self awareness. Watch your thoughts, monitor them carefully. Adopt a zero tolerance policy towards unhelpful and inaccurate thinking. Do not tolerate it. If you do not like what you are thinking, do something about it. Change that thought for a better one and practice the new view until it becomes your automatic response. Remember that you are the boss. At the end of the day, what you say goes. Take up your authority today, and guard your mind against every lie and distortion.

February 16   *Genesis 47, Nehemiah 1, Micah 4*

Talk about the Creator

Who made the heavens and the earth? Who set the planets in motion? Who engineered the universe? It is the Lord, the Almighty who set the stars in their courses. He made us all, yet many do not acknowledge Him as Creator. The evidence of His creative work surrounds them on every side (Romans 1:20), yet they do not believe that it is His work. It takes faith to believe in the non-existence of God, to deny the obvious, and there are those who have joined this religion. They have swallowed an insidious lie, intended by Satan to keep them from God. God loves them, and sends us to them. So take every opportunity to talk about the Creator to those who do not yet know Him, and pray that their eyes be opened.

February 17 *Genesis 48, Nehemiah 2, Micah 5*

Check with Heaven's wisdom

There is a saying that *'All that glitters is not gold'*. Things are not always what they seem. In fact, some things that look good, feel good, or taste good, can kill you. That is why it is vital to check things out. However intelligent or experienced you may be, it is not always easy to see what is really going on. Because there is so much you do not know, you need wisdom, especially wisdom from above. Practical wisdom can have great value, but it is only perfected by Heavenly wisdom. Walk in the light of Heaven and you will see exactly where to place your tread. This may result in choices very different to the ones you would have made, based on earthly wisdom alone. Listen to your spirit today, check, and be wise.

February 18 *Genesis 49, Nehemiah 3, Micah 6*

Follow God's map

When God shows us the place He is taking us to, He expects us to look to Him for daily direction. Some fail to do this. They are told where the path ends, but instead of going back to God for the map, they set off to find the way by themselves. This folly proves most costly, both to the well being of the person, and to the work of the Kingdom. The God who chooses the destination also shows the way to that destination. Yes, we are expected to step out, but not in presumption. This journey is by faith, from first to last! Only God knows the way. Remind yourself each morning of the place to which God has promised to take you. Then seek Him for today's directions. God has the map. Follow it!

February 19   *Genesis 50, Nehemiah 4, Micah 7*

Stop and check your bearings

Just as good navigation maintains the course of a ship, Divine guidance keeps us on God's path through life. Heaven's guidance provides the direction you need, in order to fulfil the personal mission that He has prepared for you (Ephesians 2:10). Successful navigation requires that you regularly check your position, in order to ensure that you are on track. Failure to do so can lead to loss of time and resources, or even the loss of life or mission. Therefore, it is imperative that you stop and take your bearings, as you make your journey through life. The only way to do this is to listen to God each day, and do what He says. He is your Guide for this journey, so hear, obey, and stay on course.

February 20   *Exodus 1, Nehemiah 5, Nahum 1*

Be ready for Christ's return

It has been said that the Old Testament contains more prophecies relating to Christ's second coming than to the first. Jesus' return is a Biblical certainty. When He ascended, angels announced, *"This same Jesus, who was taken up from you into heaven, will so come in like manner as you saw Him go into heaven" (Acts 1:11b).* Jesus will return on the clouds with power and great glory, and every eye will see Him. The first time He came as Saviour, to die for the sins of all. The second time He comes as King, to rule over all the earth. How can we be ready? Jesus said He would bless the 'faithful and wise servant' on His return (Matthew 24:45,46). What does this mean? It is simple: seek God and follow Him each day.

February 21　　　　　　　　*Exodus 2, Nehemiah 6, Nahum 2*

Let Him help you in exile

Sometimes people must go into exile. The Bible records such flights as that of Jacob and his family to Egypt to escape famine (Genesis 42-50), David fleeing to the Philistines to escape persecution (1 Samuel 27), and Jesus being taken out of the country by His parents to escape Herod's murderous plan (Matthew 2:13-15). In exile, Moses even named his first son Stranger, *"For he said, 'I have been a stranger in a foreign land'" (Exodus 2:22).* Great though the relief at escaping danger may be, there is also the grief of losing one's home, and the challenge of life in a different culture. It is good to know that wherever you go, *"Even there Your hand shall lead me, and Your right hand shall hold me" (Psalm 139:10).*

February 22　　　　　　　　*Exodus 3, Nehemiah 7, Nahum 3*

Feed on righteousness and health

Physical food is necessary for bodily health and strength, but there is a food that has eternal benefit to the soul. By feeding on bread and wine representing the body and blood of Christ, the entire being is strengthened! Jesus commanded that, after His death, believers would take bread and wine in memory of Him. This is the only service that Jesus gave the church It is also the greatest meal that we can ever eat in this life. When we take bread and wine in this way, we feed on righteousness and health, for His body was broken that ours would be made whole, and His blood was shed that we would be forgiven. *"Do this"* He says (Luke 22:19). So let us take bread and wine, and feed on Him by faith, with thanksgiving.

February 23   *Exodus 4, Nehemiah 8*

Enjoy joy

One of the great messages found in the eighth chapter of the book of Nehemiah is that we should turn from sorrow, for, *"The joy of the Lord is your strength" (Nehemiah 8:10)*. When he lists the fruit of the Spirit in his letter to the Galatians, Saint Paul puts joy second after love (Galatians 5:22). This joy is not limited to the transient mirth of earthly humour, fun though that may be, but something far greater, a delight of the soul that transcends our circumstances. The laughter born of this joy is eternal. Nothing can quench it! How can we experience such joy from day to day? We deepen our experience of God's joy by drawing from Him, the Source of Joy. Contemplate the God of joy. Feed on joy, until joy fills your heart!

February 24   *Exodus 5, Nehemiah 9, Habakkuk 1*

Discover what God is really like

People often wonder what God is really like. If you want to see God, look at Jesus. Jesus said, *"He who sees Me sees Him who sent Me" (John 12:45)*. Read the gospels again and again. Feed on His words, until they become part of you. You will come to know Him as a close friend whose voice you recognise. Know Jesus, and you will know God, for Jesus said, *"I and My Father are one" (John 10:30)*. Look to Jesus, for this is the path, not only to knowing what God is really like, but also to being made like God yourself – the way of deification. Christ took on our humanity that we might take on His Divinity. Let us therefore keep, *"Looking to Jesus, the author and finisher of our faith!" (Hebrews 12:2)*.

February 25   *Exodus 6, Nehemiah 10, Habakkuk 2*

Take the path to true achievement

Do not waste your precious life, but devote it to true achievement, works commissioned by Heaven. Take the path of Habakkuk. (1) **Receive** the vision: *"I will stand my watch and set myself on the rampart, and watch to see what He will say to me" (Habakkuk 2:1)*. Take your directions from God. (2) **Write** the vision: *"Then the Lord answered me and said, 'Write the vision'" (v.2a)*. Write it, so that it is clear and ever before you. (3) **Run** with the vision: *"Make it plain on tablets, that he may run who reads it" (v.2b)*. Act on it. (4) **Remain** with the vision: *"For the vision is yet for an appointed time; but at the end it will speak, and it will not lie. Though it tarries, wait for it; because it will surely come, it will not tarry" (v. 3)*. Never give up your work for God.

February 26   *Exodus 7, Nehemiah 11, Habakkuk 3*

Remember

Under the Old Covenant, God instituted festivals to remind His people of all that He had done for them. It is good to remember what God has done for you, to bring back to mind the blessings you have known. Remember the victories you have won, the blessings, the breakthroughs, the solutions, the comfort, the joy, the deliverance, and so much more that God has done for you. Give heartfelt thanks to God for these, and your soul will be greatly strengthened. Celebrate the greatness of your God! He is with you now, actively working for good in every area of your life. His grace has not come to an end. Remember His works and His faithfulness to you today, for you will again see His goodness in your life!

February 27   *Exodus 8, Nehemiah 12, Zephaniah 1*

Rejoice, for the end of deception is coming

From the day that He created humanity, God has been observing the earth, watching to see where people will place their faith, and longing that they will choose Him. All creation proclaims the reality of His existence, yet some deny the evidence, choosing to believe in unproven theory rather than in visible design. They deceive themselves who say, *"There is no God."* Worse, they deceive others also, with the lie that there can be creation without a Creator. God is against them and will topple the arrogant towers of intellectual deception in which they take refuge, and from which they seek to deceive the whole earth. Every one shall fall, and great shall that fall be. The end of deception is coming.

February 28   *Exodus 9, Nehemiah 13, Zephaniah 2*

Share in the knowledge of God

God is with us, watching from Heaven. Nothing escapes His attention. David says, *"You have searched me and known me"* (Psalm 139:1). God sees the visible and the invisible, the revealed and the hidden, the open and the closed. Moreover, He invites us to share in His knowledge. Through many kinds of revelation, including visions, dreams, prophecies, the word of knowledge, and the word of wisdom, God shares His heart and mind. Access to such privileged information is one of the many benefits that your membership of Heaven provides. You have a supernatural advantage. God calls you to seek Him, and in the stillness reveals hidden things, so that you are fully aware of all that you need to know in this life.

February 29   *Your favourite Scripture*

Choose purpose over potential

Each of us faces the challenge of submitting our human potential to our divine purpose. The mind can conceive of so much more than the body can achieve. Try to fulfil all your potential, and you will be frustrated. It is not possible to do everything you have the potential to do. You can only do so much, so focus on the work given you by Heaven. You cannot fulfil your potential, but you can fulfil your calling. That is what Jesus did. He had the ability to lead in every science and art, but He did none of those things. Instead, He subjugated all His ability to the one thing that mattered: His calling from Heaven to be the Saviour of the world. Choose purpose over potential by prioritising the work Heaven has given you.

MARCH

March 1   *Exodus 10, Zephaniah 3*

Trust God in the down times

The tide comes in, and the tide goes out. There are upturns and downturns, times of plenty and times of lack. It can be hard to trust God in the down times. It is easy to trust God when we can see wealth and resources flowing towards us, but it is not so easy when we see them being swept away! At such times we have two basic choices. We can either feed our fear, or feed our faith. Whichever one we feed will grow stronger. Fear says, *"I'm going under!"* but faith says, *"I'm going over!"* Feed your faith today. Learn to trust God in the good times and the bad. See every downturn as an opportunity to build stronger faith! By the exercise of faith, the spiritual person advances through every difficulty.

March 2   *Exodus 11, Esther 1, Haggai 1*

Learn to manage fear and anxiety

Jesus said, *"Let not your heart be troubled"* (John 14:1). Unless properly addressed, fear and anxiety can lead to feelings of powerlessness and helplessness. What can we do to manage fear most effectively? The greatest step of all is to fully place your trust in God. Faith provides certainty in an uncertain world. It comes not from assessing risk, but from assessing the claims of God, and finding that they are true. The Psalmist says, *"Taste and see that the Lord is good; blessed is the man who trusts in Him!"* (Psalm 34:8). God asks you to put Him to the test. As you trust in Him, the peace of Jesus will fill and guard your soul. Threat and danger may remain, but by God's grace you will stand!

March 3   *Exodus 12, Esther 2, Haggai 2*

Use the power of repetition

Sometimes it is important to repeat things. We may need to hear something a number of times before we remember it. Good teachers know this, and repeat key ideas to their students. God often repeats what He says to us. For example, He may often tell us that He loves us, the most important truth of all. We can apply this principle of repetition in our own inner world, by repeating to ourselves the things we most need to feed our minds upon. As we practice repeating good thoughts of God and His blessings, our mental landscape will change, becoming ever more beautiful, an inner world of peace and strength, from which love and power will flow. Use the power of repetition.

March 4   *Exodus 13, Esther 3, Zechariah 1*

Reduce the risk of the blues

Managing and mastering depression involves recognising it, identifying its causes, and applying correctives. The remedy will differ according to the cause. For example, physical causes require physical solutions. Rest may be the answer, where depression is caused by fatigue. Anti-depressant medication may be prescribed to correct a chemical imbalance in the body. Increased exercise and greater exposure to natural light are further physical changes that may be helpful. Whether or not you are depressed, you can reduce your vulnerability to depression by thinking positively, adopting a good work and leisure balance, taking regular exercise, and ensuring that you get enough rest. Reduce the risk today.

March 5   *Exodus 14, Esther 4, Zechariah 2*

Deal with life's barriers

To complete your mission from God, you will need to overcome various obstacles. Such obstacles can be very great. When the people of Israel left Egypt and came to the Red Sea, they faced a natural barrier that they could not cross. Many of them thought that they had been defeated, and their hearts sank. But Moses turned to God, who strengthened him and showed him what to do (Exodus 14:15-18). That is the key - turning to God. He alone knows the best way to deal with life's barriers. What obstacles do you face today? Ask God about them. As you daily seek His wisdom for your problems, He will show you exactly what to do. Do not be defeated by life's barriers, but overcome them in God.

March 6   *Exodus 15, Esther 5, Zechariah 3*

Look to your Source

Once upon a time there was a man who inherited a vineyard. The grapes were of exceptional quality and made wine that was renowned. Year after year, the owner worked to promote his wines, and enjoyed the wealth that his industry provided. But in his busyness there was something he did not see. The vines were slowly ageing, their yield was falling, and the quality was failing. Finally, a day came when the business collapsed. He had been so focused on the *means* of his prosperity that he had neglected its *source* – the vines. Do not rely too much on the *channels* of blessing, but rather depend daily on their *Source*, the One from whom all blessings flow. Look to your Source, and follow Him every day.

March 7   *Exodus 16, Esther 6, Zechariah 4*

Live in revival

In every revival and outpouring of the Holy Spirit, God works to change us on the inside. Because of their visibility, there is a danger that outward signs and wonders will get our attention, whilst we forget the most important part of revival, the hidden work of God in the heart. The true fruit of revival is hidden to the naked eye. We may see the effects of it, but we cannot see what God is doing on the inside. The first fruit of revival is within, and this revival takes place whenever we seek God and receive from Him. Wherever you are, you can be in revival, because revival is the outpouring of the Spirit on you. Come to Jesus and drink freely of the living water (John 7:37-39). Draw from God, and live in revival today!

March 8   *Exodus 17, Esther 7, Zechariah 5*

Use wealth rightly

To illustrate the defences in which people trust, Solomon uses the example of wealth. He says, *"The rich man's wealth is his strong city, and like a high wall in his own esteem" (Proverbs 18:11)*. Of all the things that people think might protect them, wealth is one of the most illusory. To those who use them in the service of love, riches are a great blessing, but to those who love them, they are a great curse. It is no accident that in the next line, Solomon writes, *"Before destruction the heart of a man is haughty" (v.12)*. The adjacent position of this proverb reminds us that *Arrogance* and *Riches* are common neighbours. Wealth should always be humbly held and administered as God directs. Use your wealth rightly.

March 9   *Exodus 18, Esther 8, Zechariah 6*

Do it God's way

When God gives you a vision of something to work towards, what do you do? Some make the mistake of taking what He says and trying to build it in their own way. They may think that once they have received the idea, they do not need to listen to God any more. Sadly, they neglect the very means of success: His step by step guidance. He has promised to guide us every step of the way, if we will listen. God, who gives the vision, also provides the means to accomplish it. Therefore it is imperative for the successful fulfilment of the mission that we continue to seek His daily direction. If the manufacturer of a product has provided accurate instructions for its assembly, only a fool ignores them. Do it God's way.

March 10   *Exodus 19, Esther 9, Zechariah 7*

Thank God for all His blessings

God never promises that life will be easy, even for good people. He says, *"Many are the afflictions of the righteous."* The advantage for the righteous is that, *"The Lord delivers him out of them all" (Psalm 34:19)*. David says, *"The righteous cry out, and the Lord hears, and delivers them out of all their troubles" (v.17)*. God delivers the righteous, and much more besides! When you walk with God, praising Him, seeking Him and trusting Him, He hears you (v.4), He delivers you (v.4), His angels encamp all around you (v.7), He blesses you (v.8), He meets your need (v.9), He watches over you (v.15), He guards you (v.20), He redeems you (v.22) and He justifies you (v.22). Thank God for all His blessings.

March 11   *Exodus 20, Esther 10, Zechariah 8*

Help those you can

Do not be like the selfish and greedy, who take everything they can from others. Such are despised both by God and man. Help your brother and sister. Reach out a hand of friendship and support. Tell them you will help them in any way you can. Building bonds of friendship with others is not only right but wise, for these invisible ropes may also catch you when you fall. The Bible says, *"Woe to him who is alone when he falls, for he has no one to help him up" (Ecclesiastes 4:10).* Help others, and when you are in need, call to them for help. Not all will return your favours, but some will. As Solomon says, *"A man who has friends must himself be friendly, but there is a friend who sticks closer than a brother" (Proverbs 18:24).*

March 12   *Exodus 21, Job 1, Zechariah 9*

Trust your support from Heaven

When Sennacherib king of Assyria besieged Jerusalem, Hezekiah king of Judah encouraged his people, saying, *"Be strong and courageous; do not be afraid nor dismayed before the king of Assyria, nor before all the multitude that is with him; for there are more with us than with him. With him is an arm of flesh; but with us is the Lord our God, to help us and to fight our battles"* (2 Chronicles 32:7,8). Often in life there are times when our resources are inadequate. At such times we should encourage ourselves and others with the truth that if the task was given by God, there will be more than enough support from heaven to fully succeed. Remember today, that God is with you to help you and to fight your battles. There are more with you!

March 13   *Exodus 22, Job 2, Zechariah 10*

Make God your passion

Being 'in the Spirit' is not difficult. It is just a matter of choice. Football fans do not have to make an effort to get caught up in watching their team play. Television addicts feel happier the moment their favourite programme starts. If you are interested and excited by God, you will want to be 'in the Spirit' as often as possible. Anyone who wants to live an exceptional life can. Anyone who wants to live for God can. Anyone who wants to make a difference can. The key is to do what John did: get 'in the Spirit'. If you have ever developed an interest, or a love of anything, you know how to do this. Choose meeting God as your passion, your special interest, and make time for it. The answer is in the Spirit.

March 14   *Exodus 23, Job 3, Zechariah 11*

Don't bury your anger

People often try and deal with anger by ignoring it. Some bury their anger because they believe that it is wrong to be angry. Others do so because they fear that if they allow themselves to feel anger they may lose control and do something regrettable. Whatever our reasons for burying anger, repressed anger leads to problems. Buried anger can be a powerful force that builds up pressure in the soul. Imprisoned within, it can wreak havoc with our health, or it may escape in angry outbursts that damage our work and our relationships. Do you tend to bury your anger? If so, start practising a different reaction today: admit that you are angry, share it with God, and seek His answer to it.

March 15   *Exodus 24, Job 4, Zechariah 12*

Live by design

The prophet Zechariah says that God, *"Forms the spirit of man within him" (Zechariah 12:1)*. You are not here by accident, but by design. Whether you were 'planned' by your parents or not God created you and brought you into this world. He loves you deeply, more than you know, and longs to be your Friend. Turn to Him now, for He is waiting for you, so that you can travel the journey of life together. Whether you are an old friend, or a new, if you turn to Him each day He will make you whole, enable you to fulfil your purpose in life, and welcome you in eternity. Your birth was by Divine Design, now let your life be also. Turn to Him and walk together in partnership today. What a glorious partnership that will be.

March 16   *Exodus 25, Job 5, Zechariah 13*

Find the key to being content

Saint Paul was able to say that he had learned how to be content in every situation. Coming from a man who experienced the greatest fluctuations in his material comforts, this statement reminds us that true contentment is a state of soul, rather than a material or financial condition. Lack can cause great suffering, but wealth is no guarantee of contentment. It is good when charity thrives, and wealth is distributed fairly in society, but true contentment comes from knowing that we do God's will. Isaiah teaches that there is no peace for the wicked (Isaiah 48:22). Whatever your situation, as you seek God today and do His will, His peace will fill your heart, and your soul will be content.

March 17   *Exodus 26, Job 6, Zechariah 14*

Increase your goal awareness

Do you recognise the pervasive and profound influence of goals in every area of your life? Every day we choose goals that drive our behaviour and determine to a large degree how we respond to the world around us. Our lives are full of goals (Proverbs 19:21). When we shop, we have a goal to buy what we want or need. When we work, we aim to meet some performance criteria. When we play, we want to have fun and enjoy ourselves. Goals are everywhere. How aware are you of the goals you pursue from day to day? To enjoy a higher degree of control over your life and destiny, increase your goal awareness. Practice identifying your goals today. You may spot some you have not seen before.

March 18   *Exodus 27, Job 7, Malachi 1*

Find joy and peace in believing

When asked for their views on the best way to achieve fulfilment in life, people give various answers. The Bible, in contrast, gives just one: There is no enduring peace apart from God. Carl Jung, the Swiss psychoanalyst, was one those who recognised this truth. He wrote that of all the patients he treated in the second half of his life, none were fully healed without coming into a personal relationship with God. Paul says, *"Now may the God of hope fill you with all joy and peace in believing, that you may abound in hope by the power of the Holy Spirit" (Romans 15:13).* It is *in believing* that we come to this place of peace. There is no other way but by faith. As you stand on the threshold of today, receive that peace and joy.

March 19   *Exodus 28, Job 8, Malachi 2*

Write a good letter

Much of the New Testament consists of letters inspired by the Holy Spirit, letters that inspire, enlighten, and encourage the reader. Your letters can achieve more than perhaps you think. God can speak through a letter, bringing comfort, guidance, and strength. Today we have many ways to write, including emails, texts, and pen on paper. The medium matters little, but the content matters much. Who could you bless with a letter? Pray before you write, asking God to inspire you. Then write something that will really bless them. The Holy Spirit will attend your words, and speak to the reader's heart. Only Heaven knows the influence your letter will have. When you next write to someone, make it a letter to remember.

March 20   *Exodus 29, Job 9, Malachi 3*

Teach them to listen

Oil is a biblical symbol of the Holy Spirit, and was used under the old covenant to anoint the high priest (Exodus 29:7). The pouring of the anointing oil on the head of the high priest prefigured the outpouring of the Holy Spirit on the day of Pentecost (Acts 1:8). In the Old Testament one man was anointed with oil, the symbol of the Spirit, so that he might enter the Holy Place in the temple once a year on behalf of all. But in the New Testament, everyone who desires it can receive the Holy Spirit, and enter the throne room of heaven whenever they wish! We should not only pray for others, but teach them to listen to Jesus, that they might be transformed by the Spirit, and their lives made powerful for God.

March 21   *Exodus 30, Job 10, Malachi 4*

Prepare for eternity

No one escapes justice in eternity. God sees everything and records it, pronouncing all guilty. Those who admit their sin and turn from it to Him, have their sentence waived, for Christ has paid that price on behalf of us all. You are guilty, but you go free, justified through faith in Him. But those who reject Him and His gift of life face an eternity of separation from God, and from all that is truly good. Come to God today, while there is still time. Turn to Him, but don't stop there. Do what He says, for *only* obedience will be rewarded. A day is coming when God's fire will test all you have done. *"If anyone's work is burned, he will suffer loss; but he himself will be saved, yet so as through fire"* (1 Corinthians 3:15).

March 22   *Exodus 31, Job 11, Matthew 1*

Enjoy eternal life now!

Death is not the end. God is eternal (Deuteronomy 33:27) and so are we (Matthew 25:41,46). Although we are unlike God in that we are created beings, we are like Him in that we will exist for ever. Following our earthly existence, and the last judgement, Jesus says that we will exist either in eternal fire (v.41) or in eternal life (v.46). The choice is ours. God has given us the right to choose our own eternal destiny, and He has made eternal life freely available to us now (John 5:24). Choose life today and live it to the full. Don't wait until you die to enjoy the blessings of eternal life. The life of the spirit is for you to enjoy now. Go to God and listen. Let His Spirit inspire your spirit today!

March 23   *Exodus 32, Job 12, Matthew 2*

Partner with God and fly

Walk with God and you will fly on eagle's wings (Isaiah 40:31). Your strength will be renewed and your spirit will soar as you wait on Him. Many people wonder what they can do to rise above the restraints and restrictions that hold them down. Here is the answer: put your trust in the Lord, and you will start to transcend the limitations of your earthly existence. Wait daily on Him, and you will grow stronger and fly higher. Christians who do not wait on God are like airline passengers who throw their tickets away and choose to walk instead! Personal strength and skill may get you so far, but work together with God, and His unlimited power will take you further than you ever dreamed possible.

March 24   *Exodus 33, Job 13, Matthew 3*

Go places with God

What does God want you to do today? Listen to Him and He will show you the next step in your work for Him. Stay in prayer until you know. He will lead you one step at a time. Take the next step that you can see, and He will show you the step that follows. Step by step He will lead you along the path He has chosen for you from eternity. He has planned your way, a unique path and calling, with rewards to come that are more wonderful than you can imagine. The gates to that path are wide open now. If you have wandered from it, return today. Simply look to God, and He will guide you forwards. If you have never taken that path, take it now, and make the most of the rest of your life. It's time to *really* go places!

March 25   *Exodus 34, Job 14, Matthew 4*

Feed your Spirit

In the same way that physical food is necessary for bodily health and strength, so spiritual food is vital to the health and strength of the soul. When tempted by Satan to create food during his 40 day fast in the wilderness, Jesus replied, *"It is written, 'Man shall not live by bread alone, but by every word that proceeds from the mouth of God'" (Matthew 4:4).* His reply highlights the importance that God places on hearing from Heaven. It is utterly impossible to live life to the full by dining on physical food alone. You need to feed your spirit. It is the Spirit, not the stomach that brings life. Check who is in charge: your stomach or the Spirit, and make your stomach the servant of the Spirit today.

March 26   *Exodus 35, Job 15, Matthew 5*

Be made like God

Jesus said, *"Blessed are those who hunger and thirst for righteousness, for they shall be filled" (Matthew 5:6).* This is the spiritual food that God gives to those who feed on Him. If you are hungry for all that is good, and your heart is open to God, He will fill you with Himself. It has been said of physical food that, *"We are what we eat."* If this is so physically, it is even more so spiritually. To daily feed on God is to undergo a process of deification whereby you are progressively transformed into His image (2 Corinthians 3:18). What an amazing love it is, that makes such a thing possible! *"Behold what manner of love the Father has bestowed on us, that we should be called children of God!" (1 John 3:1).*

March 27   *Exodus 36, Job 16, Matthew 6*

Trust God in difficult times

If you worry about not having enough to meet your needs, remember how Jesus said, *"Do not be anxious for your life, what you shall eat, or what you shall drink; nor for your body, what you shall put on. Is not life more than food and the body more than clothing? Behold the birds of the air; for they sow not, nor do they reap, nor gather into barns. Yet your heavenly Father feeds them; are you not much better than they are? ... But seek first the kingdom of God and all these things will be added to you"* (Matthew 6:25,26,33). If times are tough, and you are tempted to doubt that God will look after you, remind yourself that He is in charge, and that He *will* get you through. Trust Him today that He will get you what you need in time.

March 28   *Exodus 37, Job 17, Matthew 7*

Look to Heaven

Throughout His earthly ministry, Jesus instructed His hearers to, *"Repent, for the kingdom of heaven is at hand"* (Matthew 4:17). There is another world, a world in which God rules. This invisible world is closer to us than the air we breathe. We enter it by turning to God. Seek Him, and Jesus promises that your seeking will be successful. He says, *"Seek and you will find"* (Matthew 7:7). But why seek? What is the advantage? More than words can tell! Our gain is no less than life itself! We become citizens of Heaven, blessed on earth, and bound for glory. When we realise that this life is found in God alone, we reject the idols in which we once trusted, and turn eagerly to Him. The life and guidance of Heaven await you.

March 29   *Exodus 38, Job 18, Matthew 8*

Say what God says

Your words will be powerful when you say what God says. His word creates out of nothing. *"By faith we understand that the worlds were framed by the word of God, so that the things which are seen were not made of things which are visible"* (Hebrews 11:3). The centurion who came to Jesus knew the power of God's word. He said, *"Only speak a word, and my servant will be healed"* (Matthew 8:8). He knew that Jesus' word would do it. You and I have been given the same measure of faith, but we need to use it. Like the man in the story, we can go to God, hear Him, and say what He says, or we can go our own way. His word will change things for you, if you let it. Listen to God, and say what He says today.

March 30   *Exodus 39, Job 19, Matthew 9*

See as God sees

How clearly do we see things? On one occasion Jesus prayed for a blind man. The first time He prayed, the man said that he could see people, but they looked like trees walking. He had sight, but it was partial and inadequate. Jesus had to pray again before the man could see properly. Important though physical sight is, it involves more than simply the impulses that fall on the back of the retina. How we interpret those signals is a key part of perception. Two people may see the same view, but describe it quite differently. Like the blind man, we need to go to God to get an accurate view of things. We may not be blind, but we are all in the business of interpreting what we see. Get God's view on things today.

March 31   *Exodus 40, Job 20, Matthew 10*

Don't waste your time worrying

Jesus encouraged people not to worry unnecessarily. He told them to look at the lilies as clear evidence of the Father's provision (Matthew 6:25-34). The lilies, *"Neither toil nor spin"*, yet, *"Even Solomon in all his glory was not arrayed like one of these."* He also pointed to the sparrows, reminding them that, *"Not one of them falls to the ground apart from your Fathers will"* (Matthew 10:29). *"Are you not of more value?"* He said. *"If God so clothes the grass of the field, which today is, and tomorrow is thrown into the oven, will He not much more clothe you?"* (Matthew 6:30). Do not waste your precious life by pouring your energy into worry. Put it into trusting God and doing what He says. He will more than get you through.

APRIL

April 1   *Leviticus 1, Job 21, Matthew 11*

Go direct to the Source

Jesus said, "Come to Me... Take My yoke upon you and learn from Me, for I am gentle and lowly in heart, and you will find rest for your souls. For My yoke is easy and My burden is light" (Matthew 11:28-30). True success and perfect peace are found only by walking with God. There are many channels through which we may be blessed, but there is only one Source of blessing. Go direct to Him. Christianity is first and foremost a personal relationship with Christ. Do not sacrifice that for anything. Make looking to Jesus your first priority. As you do, you will find peace, and receive blessing for yourself and others. Let nothing come between you and God. Go direct to the Source today.

April 2   *Leviticus 2, Job 22, Matthew 12*

Work for heavenly recognition

How do you feel when your good motives are called into question? On earth, true value is not always recognised, and true motives often remain hidden. Only Heaven gets it right all the time. You may not receive the appreciation you deserve on earth, but do what God says and Heaven will never fail to recognise your work. Only God fully sees the true value of any act. Only the Spirit of God fully plumbs the deepest places of the human heart. He knows. Console yourself in the knowledge that God sees your good purpose and values your good work. Earth's valuations are passing, but Heaven's valuation of your work will stand forever. Seek God, and work for heavenly recognition today.

April 3   *Leviticus 3, Job 23, Matthew 13*

Hunger for the truth

Ignorance and inaccurate thinking can do a great deal of damage to our lives and relationships. To escape the prison of self-deception, we need a hunger for truth that is stronger than our love of comfort, for there are times when the truth may challenge us and demand a response. Such a hunger can drive us to God, who knows all things, and is keen to show us all that we need to know. Jesus promised that the Holy Spirit, *"Will guide you into all truth" (John 16:13)*. You do not need to know everything there is to know, but there are certain things God wants to show you about each situation. Ask the Holy Spirit to show you what you need to see, and, if you are open to it, He will show you that truth today.

April 4   *Leviticus 4, Job 24, Matthew 14*

Let duty and compassion move you

Why pray for the sick? Firstly, because it is part of the commission God gave us. It is your duty to pray for those in need. God has entrusted you and I with the ongoing ministry of His Son. Secondly, we pray because we care. Saint Paul says that, *"The love of God has been poured out in our hearts" (Romans 5:5)*. We pray because we want to. Compassion is a driving force in healing. Christ Himself was moved at the sight of the sick and suffering. Matthew reports that, *"Jesus went out and saw a great crowd, and He was moved with compassion toward them. And He healed their sick" (Matthew 14:14)*. When you see someone in need, allow duty and compassion to move you. Pray and do what you can today.

April 5   *Leviticus 5, Job 25, Matthew 15*

Enjoy Heaven's freedom

All earthly leaders have weaknesses, but the righteous government of Heaven's King is perfect. God is no tyrant, imperiously dominating His subjects and forcing them to submit, but the King of Love whose goodness never fails. Submit to Him and you will find freedom, for freedom is His nature. None are as free as those who have made the Lord their King. Many rebel against God, thinking that they will be better off by acting independently - the greatest lie of all. *"Come to Me"* He says (Matthew 11:28). Thanks to God's love, we can enjoy the benefits of Heavenly citizenship today. There are no benefits greater than these. While your heart is towards God, His grace will always be poured out upon you.

April 6   *Leviticus 6, Job 26, Matthew 16*

Read the signs of the times

Jesus criticised the people of His day because they could read natural signs, enabling them to predict the weather, but they did not read, *"The signs of the times"* (Matthew 16:3). In our own day some are overly optimistic, saying, *"Peace, peace! When there is no peace"* (Jeremiah 6:14), whilst others are overly pessimistic, seeing only doom and gloom. The Holy Spirit alone can properly interpret the signs of the times. As we walk with God and listen to Him, He will tell us all we need to know about the times we are in. If we will heed the signs, taking each one to God, who alone knows their true significance, world events will not take us unawares, and when He comes, we will be ready!

April 7   *Leviticus 7, Job 27, Matthew 17*

Manage earth from Heaven

God offers us a place of unrivalled advantage when it comes to managing our life on earth. From this place we can make the wisest decisions, speak the best words, and do the right things. This is none other than the place of friendship. The apostle Paul tells us that, *"God, who is rich in mercy, because of His great love with which He loved us, even when we were dead in trespasses, made us alive together with Christ (by grace you have been saved), and raised us up together, and made us sit together in the heavenly places" (Ephesians 2:4-6).* What a place to be. We are physically present on earth, but we have a spiritual presence with Christ, a home in heaven. God calls us to live from here, so let us seek Him and work from heaven today.

April 8   *Leviticus 8, Job 28, Matthew 18*

Draw strength from God

We cannot avoid many difficulties that life brings, but we can draw strength from the One who promises to support us through them all. Long ago, God said, *"When you pass through the waters, I will be with you; and through the rivers, they shall not overflow you" (Isaiah 43:2).* Walk with God and He will sustain you through the challenges of life. The psalmist says, *"God is our refuge and strength, a very present help in trouble. Therefore we will not fear, even though the earth be removed, and though the mountains be carried into the midst of the sea" (Psalm 46:1-2).* Whether you face poverty, loneliness, sickness, or natural disaster, He will still be there. Take heart, for, *"The Lord of hosts is with us; the God of Jacob is our refuge!" (Psalm 46:7).*

April 9   *Leviticus 9, Job 29, Matthew 19*

Love yourself

Christ commands us to love others as we love ourselves (Matthew 19:9). The first human you need to love is you. If you do not love yourself properly, you will not be able to love others properly. The healthier your self-relationship, the healthier will be your relationships with those around you. Whatever your faults and failings, you need to become your own friend. Do not deny your sin, but repent radically, and love yourself with an unshakeable love. That is how God loves you, and it is how you should love yourself. As you listen to Him each day, let the Holy Spirit show you your true self, and work with Him to develop your godly nature. Love yourself rightly, and you will be able to love others also.

April 10   *Leviticus 10, Job 30, Matthew 20*

Look ahead

If you do not look where you are going, sooner or later you will fall over. This is as true for the spirit as it is for the body. You need to walk with your spiritual eyes open, discerning the next step. Some fall because they are always looking back at the past, others because they are looking only at the end goal. Looking at the past can be helpful, as can looking ahead, but do not stay in either place. You need to keep an eye on what your feet are doing now. Focus on the present, because *that's* where you are. Look to God and live in this moment, for here you can make an impact, here you can make a difference. The present is the future becoming the past. The best time to capture the future and make history is now.

April 11   *Leviticus 11, Job 31, Matthew 21*

Receive God's grace for today

Some people see God as a distant onlooker who watches but does not care enough to intervene. The truth is very different. His love is so great that He has made the ultimate intervention on our behalf, entering the world and dying in our place so that we might escape the penalty and power of sin (John 3:16). Because of His intervention, we can be assured of eternal life simply by trusting Jesus Christ as our Lord and Saviour. Through this great intervention we receive power from heaven, the gift of the Spirit, amazing grace that is more than enough for every situation we will ever face in life. Do not wait for God to intervene. He already has. Now it is your turn. Seek God, and let Him intervene in your heart today.

April 12   *Leviticus 12, Job 32, Matthew 22*

Let God direct you

If you seek Him, God will make a way for you. It may not be what you expected, but it will always be the best route to take. Be careful not to always take the path of least resistance. Sometimes it may be right to take the easiest way, but not always. If it is, He will show you. The key is to look to Him and obey. Although the best and wisest path, God's way may not be an easy one. At times there may be great resistance, so that you must stand firm and push on through. Consider your life. Whose path are you following? Do you put your own judgement before God's? Or do you look to Him, and choose the path that He reveals to you. Whether rough or smooth, this path will lead to victory. Let God direct you.

April 13 *Leviticus 13, Job 33, Matthew 23*

Study under Christ

With a good attitude, we can learn much from study and experience. But there is a Source of learning as superior to these as diamonds are to dust: the teaching of Christ. Jesus said, *"Do not be called teachers; for One is your Teacher, the Christ" (Matthew 23:10)*. Do not let anyone take His place as your principal tutor. Some will try, so be ready to resist their claim and to submit their teaching to the judgement of God. Take counsel from Him first, for this is your inheritance. As He says: *"None of them shall teach his neighbour, and none his brother, saying, 'Know the Lord,' for all shall know Me, from the least of them to the greatest of them" (Hebrews 8:11)*. Let Him teach you, and you will learn what you most need to know.

April 14 *Leviticus 14, Job 34, Matthew 24*

Make God your business partner

Jesus says of His second coming, *"Be ready, for in that hour you think not, the Son of Man comes" (Matthew 24:44)*. He even tells us how to prepare. It is the *"faithful and wise servant"* who will be rewarded (v.45). We can prepare for that day by doing what Jesus has asked us to do. Some are busy doing their own thing 'for God', others are doing what they think God wants, but the wise stop to listen and to obey. They will have true peace while they wait for their Lord, they will be blessed when He comes (v.46), and they will reign with Christ (v.47). Time spent in prayer and seeking God is never wasted. Make God your business partner, let your first appointment each day be with Him, and let Him guide your work on earth!

April 15   *Leviticus 15, Job 35, Matthew 25*

Put the word to work

Jesus said, "To everyone who has, more will be given, and he will have abundance; but from him who does not have, even what he has will be taken away" (Matthew 25:28). This is one of Christ's sayings that people sometimes find hard to understand. He is talking about what we do with the spiritual resources that He has given us from Heaven. As we receive from Him and put His word to work, so we grow, but if we reject His gift, we are left with less than nothing. Some reject the word of God, but they can never stop it. It will simply pass them by. The blessings of that word will pass from them, and be given instead to those who are hungry for them. Be one who has. Put the word to work today.

April 16   *Leviticus 16, Job 36, Matthew 26*

Don't give up on others too soon

Following Jesus' arrest, Peter denied three times that he knew Him. Knowing Peter's weakness, Christ could have rejected him as being unsuitable for leadership. Instead He made him first leader of the church in Rome. When people let us down, or fail to come up to the standards we have set, we may be tempted to reject them. But we should take the time to pray and seek God's mind before we act. Everyone makes mistakes, but when God calls a person, He also provides all the grace they need for the role or task. All that is required is their humble reliance on Him. Do not give up on others too soon, but help them to find the place that God has chosen for them, and the grace to live for Him.

April 17   *Leviticus 17, Job 37, Matthew 27*

Switch the focus

What do you think about when you wake? Do you dwell on your problems and enter the day feeling down, or do you look to Jesus and go in feeling up? If it is the former, you need to switch your focus to Jesus. His yoke is easy and His burden light. The more you dwell on Him and listen to what He says, the brighter your spirit will shine and the better your outlook will be. The word of God changes everything that needs to be changed. The heavier your soul, the more you need to hear God's word to you. Stay as long as you need to, listening to God in prayer, until the burden lifts. Sometimes it will be sooner, but at other times you may need to pray at length before the breakthrough comes. It surely will.

April 18   *Leviticus 18, Job 38, Matthew 28*

Share your faith

In His commission, Jesus tells us to: *"Go into all the world and preach the gospel to every creature" (Mark 16:15). "Go and make disciples"* He says (Matthew 28:19). Share your faith whenever you have opportunity. There is a moment when it is appropriate to share what you believe. Sense it and seize it! Tell of how you were saved and the difference it has made in your life. But leave the Spirit to convict your hearers. Your job is to share what you have found. His job is to convert those who hear your testimony. Resist the temptation to try and do His job for Him. Far from converting others, you will more likely alienate them. Do your part and the Holy Spirit will do His. Share your faith, and God will save those who believe.

April 19   *Leviticus 19, Job 39, Mark 1*

Rely on your Friend

There are times when we all need a friend, someone to encourage us, comfort us, or just be there. That is the heart of God's command to, *"Love your neighbour as yourself" (Leviticus 19:18)*. If we all did that, no one would ever lack for a friend. Sadly, people are not always there for us when we need them, yet there is one Friend who will never desert us, the Lord Jesus Christ. He says, *"I will never leave you nor forsake you" (Hebrews 13:5)*, *"I am with you always" (Matthew 28:20)*. As the hymn writer puts it, *"What a Friend we have in Jesus!"* If we will turn to Him when we need a friend, He will find a way of comforting us. When you are down and you need a helping hand, turn to Him, and He will do what none other can do.

April 20   *Leviticus 20, Job 40, Mark 2*

Seek diligently to serve faithfully

It is clear from the Bible that God has plans for us. For example, He says to His defeated people in captivity, *"I know the thoughts that I think toward you ...thoughts of peace and not of evil, to give you a future and a hope" (Jeremiah 29:11)*. We can work with God's plans for us, or against them. Jeremiah describes how to work with God: *"And you will seek Me and find Me, when you search for Me with all your heart. I will be found by you, says the Lord, and I will bring you back from your captivity" (vv.13,14a)*. Seeking God is the foundation for serving God. As we seek Him, He directs our steps, and we follow the path He has prepared for us. You cannot enjoy God's plan without seeking His face. Seek Him today.

April 21   *Leviticus 21, Job 41, Mark 3*

Do work that lasts

If we are saved by faith, what role do good works serve in a believer's life? What difference do they make? Much in every way! Unregenerate sinners cannot stand in the presence of a holy God, but those who believe in the Lord Jesus Christ are saved. Although saved, some do nothing of eternal value. Saint Paul compares their work to wood, hay, and straw that will be burnt up. He says, *"If anyone's work is burned, he will suffer loss; but he himself will be saved" (1 Corinthians 3:15).* They will be saved, but they will have no reward. In contrast, the good work of others is compared to gold, silver and precious stones that will not be destroyed. *"If anyone's work ... endures, he will receive a reward" (1 Corinthians 3:14).*

April 22   *Leviticus 22, Job 42, Mark 4*

Trust God in the storms of life

On one occasion Jesus and His disciples needed to cross the Sea of Galilee in order to help a demonised man. He said to them, *"Let us cross over to the other side" (Mark 4:35),* and they set sail. But as they were crossing, they had to pass through a potentially life threatening situation, a great and violent storm that looked like it would sink their boat. We need to know that there are times when God leads us through crises, in order to get us to our destination. At such times we should not fear, but follow the example of Christ, whose faith enabled Him to sleep at the height of the storm. Have faith today, especially in the storms that threaten to sink your boat. Trust God that you are going over, not under.

April 23   *Leviticus 23, Psalms 1, 2, & 3, Mark 5*

Touch God in faith

The gospels record the story of a sick woman who sought to touch Jesus, that she might be healed (Mark 5:25-34). There were lots of people touching Him that day, who did not get healed, but she touched Him in a certain way. It was the touch of faith. She believed that when she touched His garment she would be healed, and so she was. Whenever we touch God in faith, power flows from Heaven. We should come to God, not merely believing that He exists, but that, *"He is a rewarder of those who diligently seek Him"* (Hebrews 11:6). As you pray today, believe that you have your answer, and in God's time and way, it will be done! Touch God in faith!

April 24   *Leviticus 24, Psalms 4, 5, & 6, Mark 6*

Pass by faith

It is said of King Hezekiah that there was a time when, *"God withdrew from him, in order to test him that He might know all that was in his heart"* (2 Chronicles 32:31). There are times in our lives when God tests us, to see what we will do. He says, *"I, the Lord, search the heart, I test the mind, even to give every man according to his ways, according to the fruit of his doings"* (Jeremiah 17:10). What does God see when He looks at your heart and mine? No one will pass the test of God on the basis of their good works. It is impossible, for all have sinned. There is only one way to pass this test: the way of faith. When we give all to Him, trusting not in our righteousness but in His love for us, seeking and doing His will, we shall pass.

April 25   Leviticus 25, Psalms 7, 8, & 9, Mark 7

Have faith in the midst of fear

Faith can banish fear, but be careful not to assume that if you are afraid you have no faith. The presence of faith does not always result in the complete absence of fear. Certainly it is good not to fear, and there were times when Jesus told people to fear not. He knew that fear can be an enemy of faith, and where this is so, its influence must be broken. But at other times, fear can be a stimulus to faith, alerting you to the need for trust in God. So the main issue is not so much the presence or absence of fear, but the presence or absence of faith. The nature of true faith is that it enables you to proceed, with or without fear. By faith we stand, often in the face of fear. What do you fear today? Hear God and have faith.

April 26   Leviticus 26, Psalms 10, 11, & 12, Mark 8

Let life and peace fill your heart

The only way to beat sin in our lives is by faith in Jesus Christ. Try to be good through your own efforts, and you will certainly fail. No one can completely keep God's law. But anyone who wants to can believe. Those who turn to God and walk with Him are justified by their faith. *"There is therefore now no condemnation to those who are in Christ Jesus, who do not walk according to the flesh, but according to the Spirit" (Romans 8:1).* Try to be perfect by following the law and you stand condemned, but follow the Spirit and you are convicted. Life and peace will fill your heart, and the surety of faith will support your life and work. Choose the life of the Spirit today, and so fulfil the righteous requirement of the law.

April 27   Leviticus 27, Psalms 13, 14, & 15, Mark 9

Listen to your moral voice

Conscience is the voice of the moral self, and guilt is the warning that we have violated our moral principles. Heed the promptings of godly conscience and you can correct your thinking and your actions. Ignore its voice and you risk eternal loss. Some break the civil law and escape justice in life, but none can break God's law and escape eternal judgement. For those who make the Lord their friend, the penalty for sin has been paid at the cross, but for those who reject His pardon, there can only be separation and darkness beyond the grave. Do not silence your conscience – let it speak. Where its guidance is of God, follow it faithfully to the end. Do what is right, and the peace of God will guard your heart today.

April 28   Numbers 1, Psalms 16, 17, & 18, Mark 10

Run into His loving arms

When little children were brought to Jesus, *"He took them up in His arms, laid His hands on them, and blessed them" (Mark 10:16).* Think of the kindest human being you know of. God is kinder. He is kinder than anyone you will ever meet. Come to Him with the simple trust of a child, and He will lift you up. Do not run *from* God, run *to* Him, for His loving arms are ever open to you. He is the Judge of the whole world, but He loves you with an everlasting love, and has made a way for love to triumph over sin, the way of the cross. Run to Him, and His loving kindness will warm, comfort, and strengthen your heart in all that is good. Come with the honesty of a small child, and His love will purify your soul and heal your heart.

April 29   *Numbers 2, Psalms 19, 20, & 21, Mark 11*

Have faith in God

Sometimes our difficulties and challenges seem irresolvable. Like immoveable mountains they tower over us, dwarfing us in their shadow. It is easy for faith to falter in the face of seemingly insurmountable barriers and insoluble problems. Responding to this challenge, Jesus encouraged His disciples to, *"Have faith in God. For truly I say to you that whosoever shall say to this mountain, 'Be removed and be cast into the sea, and shall not doubt in his heart, but shall believe that what he said shall occur, he shall have whatever he said'"* (Mark 11:23). Some problems can only be solved by faith. When you are next in an impossible situation where only a miracle will do, listen to God, pray what He says, and believe that it *will* be done!

April 30   *Numbers 3, Psalms 22, 23, & 24, Mark 12*

Turn opposition to advantage

People can lie about you, or seek to ruin your reputation, but God sees and knows the truth. Not only that, He is working for your good in all things. When the apostle Paul was falsely accused by his enemies, God so turned things around, that Paul's false accusers opened the door for him to witness to kings. Here God used the behaviour of sinful men to boost Paul's missionary achievements, bringing him before King Agrippa before sending him on to Rome where he would witness to Caesar's household. How will God turn things around for you when others oppose you unfairly or speak evil of you? Learn to trust God when you face unjust opposition. He will make sure you complete your mission.

MAY

May 1   *Numbers 4, Psalms 25, 26, & 27, Mark 13*

Face life as a conqueror

When we give our lives into the hands of God, His love will never let us go. Saint Paul says, *"For I am persuaded that neither death nor life, nor angels nor principalities nor powers, nor things present nor things to come, nor height nor depth, nor any other created thing, shall be able to separate us from the love of God which is in Christ Jesus our Lord" (Romans 8:38).* When faced with trouble, turmoil, and change, it is good to know that God's love is an enduring reality. Whatever you go through in life, God will get you through. You cannot avoid suffering, difficulty, and pain, but you can face them as a conqueror (v.37) in the strength of God's love, knowing that your bond with Him cannot be broken by anything.

May 2   *Numbers 5, Psalms 28, 29, & 30, Mark 14*

Watch

Our life on earth is spent in a spiritual war zone. Saint Peter writes, *"Be sober, be vigilant; because your adversary the devil walks about like a roaring lion, seeking whom he may devour" (1 Peter 5:8).* It is therefore absolutely necessary that we are always on our guard. One of Satan's main strategies from the beginning has been to capture the heart through the mind. He tried this with the first humans and won, but when he tried the same trick on Jesus he was utterly defeated. Jesus told his disciples to, *"Watch and pray, lest you enter into temptation. The spirit indeed is willing, but the flesh is weak" (Mark 14:38).* So, be vigilant. Those who adopt an attitude of watchfulness will be more than ready to resist his lies and see him flee.

May 3 *Numbers 6, Psalms 31, 32, & 33, Mark 15*

Remember God is there

There can be times when it feels as though God is absent, or at least a long way away. Disappointment, fatigue, and depression are three of the states that can make us vulnerable to feeling like this. Knowing that we will have such feelings, God says clearly, *"I will never leave you nor forsake you" (Deuteronomy 31:6; Hebrews 13:5)*. We cannot guarantee that we will always *feel* God's presence, but we can guarantee the *fact* of His presence with us. Unlike changeable feelings, *"The counsel of the Lord stands forever" (Psalm 33:11)*. Jesus says, *"I am with you always" (Matthew 28:20)*. When it feels as though God is not there, remember the facts: He is with you every moment of the day.

May 4 *Numbers 7, Psalms 34, 35, & 36, Mark 16*

Ask God to act on your behalf

How do you react when others oppose you wrongfully? When David was in this situation he faced those, *"Who are wrongfully my enemies" (Psalm 35:19)*, who opposed him (v.1), who pursued him (v.3), who sought to kill him (v.4), who tried to trap him (v.7), who wanted to rob him (v.10), who spread lies about him (v.11), who repaid him evil for good (v.12), who rejoiced in his adversity (v.15), who mocked him (v.16), and who devised deceitful schemes against him (v.20). David turned to God and asked Him to act on his behalf: *"This You have seen, O Lord; do not keep silence ... Stir up Yourself, and awake to my vindication ... Let them be ashamed and brought to confusion who rejoice at my hurt" (vv.22-28)*.

May 5   *Numbers 8, Psalms 37, 38, & 39, Luke 1*

Don't envy the wicked

It is disturbing to see the wicked prosper and there may be times when we are tempted to envy their undeserved success (Psalm 73:3). They may be successful now, but David reminds us that the prosperity of the wicked is a short-lived illusion. He says, *"Do not fret because of evildoers, nor be envious of the workers of iniquity. For they shall soon be cut down like the grass, and wither as the green herb" (Psalm 37:1)*. However clever, their plans will all eventually fail, for, *"The Lord brings the counsel of the nations to nothing; He makes the plans of the peoples of no effect" (Psalm 33:10)*. In contrast, *"The counsel of the Lord stands forever" (v.11)*. The prosperity of those who seek God and follow His counsel is a permanent reality.

May 6   *Numbers 9, Psalms 40, 41, & 42, Luke 2*

Keep an eternal perspective

The only way to see the true value of things is to view them from eternity. When you trust in Christ, He gives you citizenship of Heaven, and sits you with Him in heavenly places (Ephesians 2:6). Although you still live on earth, you now have a spiritual place in Heaven. Heaven is your home, and you are temporarily resident on earth. Because of this, you have the ability to see things from a heavenly viewpoint and by so doing you can assess their true value. But if you forget your home country and adopt the ungodly values of earth, your clear vision will fail, your good judgement will be clouded, and your work will become increasingly worthless. The best view is from Heaven, so keep an eternal perspective!

May 7   *Numbers 10, Psalms 43, 44, & 45, Luke 3*

Paint an accurate self portrait

How do you see yourself? Your self-concept exerts a powerful influence on your experience and behaviour. It is made up of all your ideas about yourself, such as your view of who and what you are, your evaluation of your worth, your estimation of your capabilities, and your image of who and what you would like to be. Many elements combine to form this complex picture. This self portrait may be a more or less faithful likeness. It may be painted with photographic realism, or it may represent not so much the self as it is, but what you would like it to be. Your challenge is to paint an accurate and helpful picture of yourself. Believe what God says about you, and your self-concept will be accurate.

May 8   *Numbers 11, Psalms 46, 47, & 48, Luke 4*

Be still

Many think that activity is the greatest key to living life most fully, but this is not God's primary emphasis. He says, *"Be still, and know that I am God!" (Psalm 46:10).* Stillness, not activity, is the foundation for abundant living. There is a place of stillness that may be found even in the midst of turmoil, trouble, and change. This is an inner place reached by an inward journey. It is not the withdrawal of the neurotic to a place of escape, but the advance of the wise to a place of power. Enter here, and you will find all you need to manage your life, in both the rough times and the smooth. Live here, and your activity will be fruitful. Work from here, and your life will be ordered by Heaven. Enter the stillness today.

May 9   *Numbers 12, Psalms 49, 50, & 51, Luke 5*

Ask for help from others as God directs

It is good to be capable and resourceful, but not to be so independent that we never ask for help when we need it. There are times when it is right to ask others for assistance. Some mistakenly think that if you are trusting God, you should not ask help from others. This is nonsense. The gospels tell of a time when Jesus told the disciples to go fishing, despite the fact that they had been fishing all night and caught nothing. They obeyed and the fishing trip was an outstanding success. In fact, they caught so many fish that the net was breaking. So, *"They signalled their partners, those in the other boat, to come and help them. And they came and filled both the boats" (Luke 5:7)*. When you need help from others, ask.

May 10   *Numbers 13, Psalms 52, 53, & 54, Luke 6*

Choose faith, not fear

When Moses sent spies to reconnoitre the Promised Land, all twelve saw the same things. However, ten of them thought very differently about what they saw to the other two. They said, *"'We are not able to go up against the people, for they are stronger than us,' and they brought an evil report of the land" (Numbers 13:31,32)*. Their doubt cost them their lives in the wilderness. In contrast, Caleb and Joshua, had faith that it could be done. Caleb said, *"Let us go up at once and possess it, for we are well able to overcome it" (v.30)*. What will you choose? The faithless attitude of the ten that made them afraid and kept them from God's promise, or the faith of the two that made them confident and led to their blessing?

May 11   *Numbers 14, Psalms 55, 56, & 57, Luke 7*

Dare to believe

God calls each of us to a particular path through life, directing our steps as we listen to Him from day to day. There will be times when His directions will challenge us, stretching our faith and taking us to new and higher levels. So it was for the twelve spies that Moses sent to look at the Promised Land (Numbers 13 & 14). Only two chose to believe that with God they could enter the land, and they did indeed enter. Like the woman who anointed Jesus' feet with fragrant oil (Luke 7:36-50), they dared to believe. Dare to believe that whatever God calls you to do, can be achieved with His help. Stand on the foundation of His word, the strongest foundation of all, and say, *"It will be done!"*

May 12   *Numbers 15, Psalms 58, 59, & 60, Luke 8*

Rest in the storm

The Gospels tell of a time when Jesus and His disciples were crossing the sea and a violent storm arose, threatening to sink them (Luke 8:22-25). What did Jesus do? He slept. Why? He slept because He had confidence that they would arrive safely. This is the rest of faith, spoken of by the writer of Hebrews, who says: *"We who have believed do enter into rest" (Hebrews 4:3)*. What did the disciples do in this situation? They panicked. Why? Because they doubted that they would arrive safely. In fact, they thought they would drown. So Christ asked them, *"Where is your faith?" (Luke 8:25)*. Where is *your* faith today? If you obey Jesus, then He is in your boat, and you will make it. Trust God, and rest in the storm.

May 13   *Numbers 16, Psalms 61, 62, & 63, Luke 9*

Choose the most brilliant strategy

Godly goals are great, but achieving them requires a strategy. A strategy is a plan for achieving a given objective. God is the ultimate Strategist. Only a being of infinite intelligence could manage the incredibly complex interaction of factors involved in the operation of the universe, and only a being of infinite love could do so in a way that preserves the freedom of the human will, whilst at the same time guaranteeing the final triumph of justice and righteousness. When we go to God for guidance, we are directed according to the most brilliant strategy. As we faithfully do what He says, the goals He gave us are achieved. Do not waste your valuable time and energy. Let the Divine Strategist direct you today.

May 14   *Numbers 17, Psalms 64, 65, & 66, Luke 10*

Do the one thing that is needed

Much is written about managing time, but little is said about the greatest time management principle of all. If you are wise enough to implement it, this first rule of time management will so dramatically revolutionise your life that you will accomplish more than is possible using any other time management approach or technique. Not only will you achieve the most, but what you do will be the best. No other principle yields results like this. This remarkable and unique principle is so simple, yet many overlook it. It is the practice of seeking God in all things. Make this your habit, starting today, and you will see the supernatural results for yourself. *"One thing is needed"* says Jesus (Luke 10:42), and this is it.

May 15   Numbers 18, Psalms 67, 68, & 69, Luke 11

Forgive

Jesus teaches us to pray, *"Forgive us our sins, for we also forgive everyone who is indebted to us" (Luke 11:4)*. Because of sin's corrupting influence, it is vital that we are forgiven, and that we forgive others. When received or given, forgiveness heals, purifying the soul from sin's poison. Do not wait to receive forgiveness. The doors of Heaven will remain locked until you do. And do not wait to grant forgiveness. Wait for an apology and you may wait forever! Some may apologise, but not all. We who have been freely forgiven by God have no right to withhold forgiveness from another. You did not deserve forgiveness, but God forgave you, and you received it. Love like Him, and extend the same grace to others.

May 16   Numbers 19, Psalms 70, 71, & 72, Luke 12

Catch the fire!

When the French mathematician Blaise Pascal encountered God, he expressed his experience by repeating one word: *"Fire!"* The writer of Hebrews says, *"Our God is a consuming fire" (Hebrews 12:29)*. The Fire refines and purifies, eternally destroying all that is evil. No sin can remain in His presence. His love burns as a fire that can never be quenched. Fire was the purpose of Jesus' mission. He said, *"I came to send fire on the earth, and how I wish it were already kindled! (Luke 12:49)*, and on the Day of Pentecost the fire from Heaven fell. As we walk with God, we will catch the fire. It will burn within us, for He makes His ministers *"a flame of fire" (Hebrews 1:7)*. As at Pentecost, so today, fire!

May 17   *Numbers 20, Psalms 73, 74, & 75, Luke 13*

Work with your failures

Nobody likes to fail, yet failure is indigenous to a fallen world. We either work with it, or forgo success, for success often comes only after the lessons of failure have been learnt. Even God works with failure. His great project of creation failed when sin invaded earth, bringing bondage to death and decay. Yet God did not reject His creation, but came in person to deliver it, carrying our sin and turning defeat to victory. Never was greater success wrought than on that day. Death came through Adam's failure, but life through Christ's success. Jesus models how to deal with failure: submit to the Father's will! God has a plan for us to follow, that will turn failure to success. Follow Him, and work with your failures.

May 18   *Numbers 21, Psalms 76, 77, & 78, Luke 14*

Keep God as your Source

God, "Gives us richly all things to enjoy" (1 Timothy 6:17), but we must be careful not to put any of these in the place that He alone should hold in our heart. God knows that, being finite, we will necessarily be dependent on many things, but our primary trust must be in Him. As we come to depend on things, there is always a danger that we may lean too much on them, so that they take His place in our life and we trust them more than Him. Check your primary trust. When you put someone or something else in first place, it is idolatry, and you will lose the peace of God. We all battle with this, which is why it is good to repent daily of our misplaced dependency, and turn back to God, our one and only Source.

May 19   *Numbers 22, Psalms 79, 80, & 81, Luke 15*

Submit your conscience to God

God and Satan are not the only ones who seek to guide our moral choices. Conscience is shaped by many influences, including those of parents, teachers, friends, and society. Conscience tells us what we should or should not do. Some see it as an infallible guide to righteous living. *"Just follow your conscience,"* they say. If only they knew how biased this guide can be! Many have suffered at the hands of those whose sense of right and wrong was distorted. In moral decision making, God's guidance should always take precedence over conscience. A conscience renewed by the Holy Spirit will serve us well, but even that should be submitted to God. Follow God in all your moral choices.

May 20   *Numbers 23, Psalms 82, 83, & 84, Luke 16*

Learn God's ways

Moses says of the King, that God's law, *"Shall be with him, and he shall read it all the days of his life, that he may learn to fear the Lord his God and be careful to observe all the words of this law"* (Deuteronomy 17:19). Isaiah says, *"Learn to do good"* (Isaiah 1:17). God has many things to teach us, but will we listen? Many are trained by others, some are self-taught, but wise is he who makes God his teacher. To daily walk with God is to benefit from the greatest education available in this life. The humble soul that delights in truth will quickly learn His ways. The diligent student who daily attends God's school will gain the heights of wisdom. Do not miss out on your education. Listen to the Teacher, and learn from Him today.

May 21   *Numbers 24, Psalms 85, 86, & 87, Luke 17*

Step out in faith

In the story of the ten lepers who asked Jesus to heal them, we read that, *"He said to them, 'Go, show yourselves to the priests.' And so it was that as they went, they were cleansed"* (Luke 17:14). They were healed *"as they went"*. There are some things in life that only happen as you go. There are times when we have to take a step before things start to change. Preparation is helpful, but sometimes we try to prepare too much before we set out on the path. Some want all their questions answered before they go. Others want to ensure zero risk. Yet more want to know everything that will happen in advance. When God says, *"Go!"* it is time to go. Do not delay. Put action to your faith, for things will happen as you go.

May 22   *Numbers 25, Psalms 88, 89, & 90, Luke 18*

Persist in prayer for the sick

When you pray for the sick do not give up at the first sign of difficulty. Whilst some are healed instantly, others are healed slowly over a period of days, weeks, months, or even years. Repeated prayer may be needed before the desired results are seen. Even Christ had to pray twice on at least one occasion. We should therefore pray for as long as it takes. Jesus taught that, *"It is always right to pray and not to faint"* (Luke 18:1). Sometimes we may be tempted to give up, but unless God says to stop, we should stand firm, remembering that we are called to be, *"Imitators of those who through faith and patience inherit the promises"* (Hebrews 6:12). Keep praying, as directed by the Lord, until He says to pray no more. Persist in prayer!

May 23   *Numbers 26, Psalms 91, 92, & 93, Luke 19*

Dwell in the secret place

The Psalmist says, *"He who dwells in the secret place of the Most High shall abide under the shadow of the Almighty. I will say of the Lord, 'He is my refuge and my fortress; my God, in Him I will trust'" (Psalm 91:1,2)*. Your communion with God is a secret place that no one can take from you, and in which you will be resourced with everything you need to live your life for Him. Dwell in that place and He will look after you, *"Keep you in all your ways" (v.11)*, and, *"Be with you in trouble" (v.15)*. There is no greater Friend and Helper than the Almighty, so stay close to Him. Some enter the secret place from time to time, but the best thing is never to leave it. This is the place to dwell. Base your life here, in communion and trust.

May 24   *Numbers 27, Psalms 94, 95, & 96, Luke 20*

Let your concerns be healthy

Unhealthy anxiety sees threats but fails to hear God's word about them. Healthy anxiety, in contrast, sees the same threats, but looks to God and believes His word. This is the kind of helpful concern that Paul experienced daily over the welfare of the churches, referring to his *"deep concern"* for them (2 Corinthians 11:28). Do you have an anxiety over which you have not yet sought God? Go to Him now and listen for His answer. Do not stay in the place of unhealthy anxiety, but move to a place of faith, where even the deepest concern can never displace the peace of God that passes all understanding. As David says, *"In the multitude of my anxieties within me, Your comforts delight my soul" (Psalm 94:19)*.

May 25   *Numbers 28, Psalms 97, 98, & 99, Luke 21*

Make up a new song

"*Oh, sing to the Lord a new song! For He has done marvellous things; His right hand and His holy arm have gained Him the victory*" *(Psalm 98:1).* In a world of pain and suffering, it is easy to lose sight of God's goodness. Do not get fixated on the devil's work, but stop regularly to think of all the marvellous things that the Lord has done for you, and then turn it into a song. Make up a new song, your own song, and sing it to God. Don't worry too much about how it sounds. In your private worship you do not have to be a good singer! It is your heart that matters most. Sing from the heart. Sing out your praise to God! Sing as loud as you like, for as long as you like. Why not make up a new song right now?

May 26   *Numbers 29, Psalms 100, 101, & 102, Luke 22*

Do this

When Christ shared His last meal with the disciples, he gave directions for a great celebration that was to take place regularly after his death. It was to be a simple meal consisting of bread and wine, eaten in memory of His sacrifice. Taking bread in His hands, He said, "*This is My body which is given for you; do this in remembrance of Me*" *(Luke 22:19),* and taking a cup, He said, "*This cup is the new covenant in My blood, which is shed for you*" *(v.20).* No celebration on earth is as glorious. Only Heaven has a greater, and that is the celebration prefigured by this one: the marriage supper of the Lamb. Jesus invites you to take bread and wine in remembrance of Him today.

May 27　　　　　*Numbers 30, Psalms 103, 104, & 105, Luke 23*

Stand firm against wrongful opposition

It is impossible to truly serve God on earth without opposition. When others oppose you, check out your mandate with God. If you have got His support, then stand firm. It has been rightly said that, *"One person with God is in the majority."* But do not stop there. Stay in prayer, because you need to know how to handle the opposition. God the Master Strategist will show you what to do. He will give you a tailor made plan from Heaven, directions wiser than any the human mind could advise. Do not give up on the inside, but stand firm, holding fast to the truth by faith in your heart. Strengthen your weak knees and stand, for God is standing with you. Follow His orders and glorify Him.

May 28　　　　　*Numbers 31, Psalms 106, 107, & 108, Luke 24*

Take Heaven's medicine

Those of us who have access to the benefits of modern medicine are very grateful for the relief it provides. But we recognise that, however advanced our medical science, God is still the Source of healing. The Bible says of God that, *"He sent His word and healed them"* (Psalm 107:20). God has a word for you in your sickness, whatever that sickness is. It is a message that carries His healing power. That word will heal you in some way, if you receive it with a soft and believing heart. God has a health-building message for you today. To find out what it is, take time to pray and listen to Him. Ask Him what He is saying to you in your sickness, and then take your medicine from Heaven!

May 29   Numbers 32, Psalms 109, 110, & 111, John 1

Walk in the true Light

Saint John says of Christ that, *"In Him was life, and the life was the light of men" (John 1:4)*. He was, *"The true Light which gives light to every man coming into the world" (v.9)*. People often talk of 'seeing things in a different light' to describe experiences that lead them to change their viewpoint. As the true Light, Jesus Christ is the only one who can illuminate your heart and mind with all truth. Walk with Him each day, and His agent, the Holy Spirit, whom He poured out on the Day of Pentecost, will lead you into all truth. Be careful to test what you hear from human sources. People are all subject to bias. Take the matter to the Lord in prayer, and let Him lead you in the truth. Walk in the true Light, and your steps will be sure!

May 30   Numbers 33, Psalms 112, 113, & 114, John 2

Let God guide your ministry

Let God guide you when you pray for the sick. Listen to Him on behalf of the sick person. If He directs you in specific ways, follow those directions. The potential diversity of healing ministry is richly illustrated in the Old and New Testament accounts of healing. In the Bible, God uses many different means to heal, including steps as diverse as heartfelt prayer (2 Kings 20:5), bathing in a river seven times (2 Kings 5:10), being anointed with mud (John 9:6), having hands laid on one (Luke 4:40), or being commanded to be well (Acts 3:6). Mary's advice remains the guiding principle: *"Whatever He says to you do it" (John 2:5)*. Simply listen and obey. God will show you what to do.

May 31 Numbers 34, Psalms 115, & 116, John 3

Celebrate life!

Paul tells us that, *"The last enemy that will be destroyed is death" (1 Corinthians 15:26).* Death is an enemy we must all face. Yet many face death unprepared. People do not like to think about death, with the result that they often fail to prepare. Many are more concerned to plan holidays than to plan for beyond the grave. Death is not the end, but a transition to eternity, spent either with God or separated from Him. The choice is ours. God has made eternal life available now, and invites us to come and receive it. Jesus says that, *"God so loved the world that He gave His only begotten Son, that whoever believes in Him should not perish but have everlasting life" (John 3:16).* Choose life, but don't stop there. Live your life to the full!

June

June 1   Numbers 35, Psalms 117, & 118, John 4

Finish His work

Jesus said, *"Do not labour for the food which perishes, but for the food which endures to everlasting life" (John 6:27).* Yes, we must work to pay our bills, but is that our only motive? Is there not a much higher purpose? Should not the primary purpose of work be to do the will of God? Jesus said, *"My food is to do the will of Him who sent Me, and to finish His work" (John 4:34).* He daily looked to the Father and did what the Father showed Him to do. This is our model, our pattern. Whatever our role, trade, or profession, if we will daily seek God and follow His directions, our work will change. It will become the work of heaven on earth, a sublime endeavour rather than a mundane chore, as we labour knowing that we do God's will.

June 2   Numbers 36, Psalm 119, John 5

Let God write on your heart

The history of written media has seen a progressive decline in the permanence of records. Written records have moved from the relative indestructibility of stone tablets, to weaker clay tablets, to less solid papyrus, to the flimsiness of paper, and finally to vast electronic records that can be lost in a moment! In contrast, the records of God can never be destroyed, for they are inscribed on human hearts. As Paul explains, *"You are an epistle of Christ, ministered by us, written not with ink but by the Spirit of the living God, not on tablets of stone but on tablets of flesh, that is, of the heart" (2 Corinthians 3:3).* Give the tablet of your heart to God today, that He may write what He will. Let the permanent record show that your life was lived in Him.

June 3   *Deuteronomy 1, Psalms 120, 121, & 122, John 6*

Feast on God

What is the greatest spiritual food of all? Jesus' answer is clear: *"Most assuredly, I say to you, unless you eat the flesh of the Son of Man and drink His blood, you have no life in you. Whoever eats My flesh and drinks My blood has eternal life, and I will raise him up at the last day. For My flesh is food indeed, and My blood is drink indeed" (John 6:53-55).* Just as bodily health depends on a balanced diet, and mental health requires that we feed on constructive thoughts, so spiritual health is only possible when we feast on God. This supernatural diet, uniquely illustrated by the Christian service of communion or mass, is the staple diet of the saints. Do not go hungry. Feast on Christ today. Seek Him, and He will marvellously feed your soul.

June 4   *Deuteronomy 2, Psalms 123, 124, & 125, John 7*

Believe and be filled

Deep in the heart of every human being there is a hunger and a thirst so strong that it is the primary driver of all human behaviour and experience. This need is the foundation of all human motivation. It is the primary longing that drives humankind, and yet there is nothing this world can provide that will fully satisfy it. Christ, the father of all true psychology (and so much more!) once said, *"If anyone thirsts, let him come to Me and drink. He who believes in Me, as the Scripture has said, out of his heart will flow rivers of living water" (John 7:37,38).* Many things in life can make you feel good, but only one thing can make you fully whole! Believe and be filled today.

June 5   *Deuteronomy 3, Psalms 126, 127, & 128, John 8*

Be free

Jesus once said to some of the first Jewish believers, *"If you abide in My word, you are My disciples indeed. And you shall know the truth, and the truth shall make you free"* (John 8:31,32). We should never underestimate the power of Jesus' words to transform our lives. They are the revelation of truth that sets us free! Our spiritual diet therefore, should be rich in His word. The words He speaks to us will be the most important ones we hear in this life. If we are wise, we will feast on the words of Christ in the gospels, and on the words He speaks to us directly, as we meditate on Him each day. As you take His word to heart and live by it, the truth will make you free indeed!

June 6   *Deuteronomy 4, Psalms 129, 130, & 131, John 9*

Stand firm in difficulty

Jesus said, *"The night is coming when no one can work"* (John 9:4). There are times in life when it is hard to get anything done. For example, you may be fighting sickness, opposition, or lack of resources. Such times can be frustrating, and you may even be tempted to give up. But if you are doing God's work, stand firm. When you are next in this situation, remind yourself that although you may be facing a storm of difficulty right now, there has never been a storm that did not pass! This storm will blow over, and when it does, you will still be standing. The storm will be followed by calm, night will be followed by day, and if there is more work for you to do, you will take up your work again. Always stand firm in difficulty.

June 7   *Deuteronomy 5, Psalms 132, 133, & 134, John 10*

Take the role God has given you

During Jesus' earthly ministry, it was said by many that, *"John did no miracle, but all the things that John spoke of this Man were true" (John 10:41).* John's role was to prepare the way for Jesus, and he was faithful to follow it, preaching the truth and pointing the way. Then Jesus came, preaching, teaching, and doing miracles. If John had done miracles, Jesus' ministry might have had much less impact. Sometimes other people's callings may look more attractive, and we may be tempted to copy them, but God will not reward that which He did not request. There is no more glorious calling than the one He has given you. Stick to it like glue. Reject the rest, take up the role God has given you, and give it your all today.

June 8   *Deuteronomy 6, Psalms 135, 136, & 137, John 11*

Follow wholly

When it comes to your relationship with God, what kind of a follower are you? God says, *"You shall love the Lord your God with all your heart, with all your soul, and with all your strength" (Deuteronomy 6:5).* Mary says, *"Whatever He says to you, do it" (John 2:5).* God detests half-heartedness. Caleb the spy is rewarded, *"Because he wholly followed the Lord" (Deuteronomy 1:36),* whilst others fail to receive what was promised them *"Because they have not wholly followed Me" (Numbers 32:11).* Failure to do all that God says will cost us dear. Therefore we should follow God to the uttermost! Whenever you discover that you have fallen short, turn back to Him in repentance and faith. Those who follow wholly will be rewarded richly.

June 9   *Deuteronomy 7, Psalms 138, 139, & 140, John 12*

Seek first the Kingdom

God is not far from any of us, which is why the psalmist says, *"Where shall I go from Your Spirit? Or where shall I flee from Your presence? If I go up into Heaven, You are there; if I make my bed in Sheol, behold, You are there. If I take the wings of the morning and dwell in the furthest parts of the sea; even there shall Your hand lead me, and your right hand shall hold me"* (Psalm 139:7-10). When Jesus said, "The kingdom of heaven is at hand" (Matthew 4:17), He was showing that God is near and may be found by those who turn to Him. You do not have to travel to find God. He is with you now, wherever you are. If you turn to Him and listen, He will speak with you and show you what to do each day. *"Seek first the kingdom of God"* (Matthew 6:33).

June 10   *Deuteronomy 8, Psalms 141, 142, & 143, John 13*

Let the word wash you clean

At the Last Supper, Jesus not only shared bread and wine with His disciples. He washed their feet (John 13:1-17). It is mostly through our feet that we physically connect with the earth. If we walk with Jesus, He will cleanse us from all the dirt that clings to our soul as we walk through this world. It is impossible to walk on earth and not have contact with its corruption and sin, but Christ washes our feet. To walk with Him is to walk in righteousness and truth. No dirt can resist the cleansing power of His word. As you walk with Him, His word washes you clean from all unrighteousness. You are a member of the invisible church, the spotless Bride of Christ, awaiting His return with unshakeable confidence.

June 11 *Deuteronomy 9, Psalms 144, 145, & 146, John 14*

Look forward to your heavenly home

On one occasion when Jesus taught His disciples about the afterlife, He said, *"In My Father's house are many mansions. If it were not so, I would have told you. I go to prepare a place for you"* (John 14:2). God knows how important it is for us to have a strong sense of eternal security. Having a home adds significantly to our well being, and if our home is under threat we will be anxious. Jesus makes it clear that those who walk with Him will have a mansion for a home in Heaven. If you have ever seen a beautiful house on earth, it will not compare with your house in eternity. The architecture, the decor, the aspect, will all be prepared personally for you by your Father. Look forward to your heavenly home.

June 12 *Deuteronomy 10, Psalms 147, 148, & 149, John 15*

Commit your losses to God

Lose something or someone important to you, and you are likely to feel sad. Sadness is a response to real or perceived loss. Generally, the more we valued what was lost, the greater our sorrow will be. In a fallen world, marred by death and decay, loss will never be far away. Some respond to loss by burying uncomfortable feelings of sadness, whilst others fuel their grief so that it consumes them. Sadness should be faced and felt, but never fed. It is enough as it is. When sad, we should seek that which may be regained, or grieve that which cannot be. If this is not clear, God will show you. Commit whatever you lose to Him, and get His word on it, the only word that will bring comfort and peace to your soul.

June 13   *Deuteronomy 11, Psalm 150, John 16*

Seek truth

Moses says, *"Take heed, lest your heart be deceived, and you turn aside and serve other gods and worship them" (Deuteronomy 11:16)*. Truth is the inoculation against deception. Seek truth, pursue it. For truth brings lasting freedom. Choose to live in the light of Divine reality, rather than to be fooled by human rhetoric. Shun perceptual biases and partiality, knowing that these are the enemies of liberty and justice. Be a radical seeker of truth, and truth will reward you with freedom. Jesus promised that the Holy Spirit will guide us into all truth (John 16:13). Walk with God, and the light of truth will shine brightly in your soul, dispelling the darkness of lies and deception. Turn on the light today.

June 14   *Deuteronomy 12, Proverbs 1, & 2, John 17*

Reject the illusion of concern

There is a point in Ezekiel's life when God reveals to him the true condition of his listeners. He says, *"They come to you as people do, they sit before you as My people, and they hear your words, but they do not do them; for with their mouth they show much love, but their hearts pursue their own gain" (Ezekiel 33:31)*. Here the Holy Spirit exposes the illusion of concern. He does this so that we can turn from hypocrisy, and show sincere concern from a true heart. He also does it to show us those who are not what they seem, so that we are no longer taken in by clever rhetoricians, those who pretend to care but instead are motivated by self-interest. The illusion of concern is an enemy of individuals, churches and nations. Reject it!

June 15   *Deuteronomy 13, Proverbs 3, John 18*

Identify your hidden defences

Failure to seize opportunities because we are anxious is a defensive reaction that can rob us of happiness and success. Unchallenged, such reactions often become stronger. Used repeatedly, they become established parts of our life management repertoire, creating a psychological prison from which it may be difficult to escape. If you regularly use a particular defensive response, your use of it will become increasingly automatic, so that you become less and less conscious of what you are doing. Identifying and unlocking your hidden defences therefore becomes an imperative. Only the Holy Spirit can fully search the heart. Ask Him today to show you your hidden defences. He will.

June 16   *Deuteronomy 14, Proverbs 4, John 19*

Get wisdom

Solomon says, *"Get wisdom! Get understanding! ... Do not forsake her, and she will preserve you; love her, and she will keep you. Wisdom is the principal thing; therefore get wisdom"* (*Proverbs 4:5-7*). There is none wiser than the person who consistently listens to God. The fear of the Lord is the beginning of wisdom. This is where it starts. The Source of all true wisdom is with you. Listen diligently to Him and you will become wise. He will show you many things that you would not otherwise see, hidden things. God has given you the Spirit of wisdom and understanding, for this is His Spirit, but you must listen. Ignore the Spirit, and you remain a fool. Heed the Spirit's guidance, and you will become wise.

June 17   *Deuteronomy 15, Proverbs 5, John 20*

Recognise your uncertainties

Human beings tend to have a low tolerance of ambiguity and uncertainty. We like things to be clear, especially matters we consider important. Uncertainty and value are the two psychological ingredients of anxiety. We see both in Mary's concerned reaction to the empty tomb on the Resurrection morning. She says, *"They have taken away the Lord ... and we do not know where they have laid Him" (John 20:2)*. If you have a hope, a desire, a goal, or an expectation that is important to you, but you are not sure it will be met, anxiety will result. When you are anxious, look to see what you are uncertain of. By this means you will soon become able to explain many of the specific anxieties you feel.

June 18   *Deuteronomy 16, Proverbs 6, John 21*

Face and feel your anger

It is important for our health and well being that we face and feel our anger. That is why Paul says, *"'Be angry, and do not sin': Do not let the sun go down on your wrath" (Ephesians 4:26)*. If we are angry, integrity requires that we face it. God would rather we were honest about how we feel, than pretend that we are not angry. Sometimes anger is appropriate, but even righteous anger needs to be properly managed. Do not let the day end without addressing your anger. Face it, feel it, and listen to what God has to say about it. The Lord will have a word for you that will help you to manage the anger in the best possible way. Keep practising this positive response to anger, until you master it.

June 19 *Deuteronomy 17, Proverbs 7, Acts 1*

Let the power from Heaven loose

As we walk with God from day to day, trusting in Him, listening to Him, and following His guidance from Heaven, we are filled with the Holy Spirit. Immediately prior to His Ascension, Jesus said, *"You shall be baptised with the Holy Spirit not many days from now" (Acts 1:5)* and *"You shall receive power when the Holy Spirit has come upon you" (Acts 1:8)*. He was referring to what was about to take place on the Day of Pentecost. On that great day, God poured out the Holy Spirit on all those who believe. Repent of your sin, and lean wholly on God today. Diligently seek Him with a humble heart, and His Spirit will inspire and empower you in the life to which you have been called. Let the power from Heaven loose!

June 20 *Deuteronomy 18, Proverbs 8, Acts 2*

Continue the work of Christ

Jesus is as committed to healing today as He was during the days of His earthly ministry. Whilst on earth He healed all kinds of diseases, and all the sick that came to Him. He promised that following His ascension and the outpouring of the Holy Spirit, His followers would be empowered to carry on His healing ministry. He said, *"Whatever you ask in My name, I will do it," (John 14:13)*. Will you take up the ministry He bequeathed? Answer the call to heal, and the Lord will train you. He is the Healer, and He will heal through you, if you are willing and obedient. Take your place today amongst those who pray for the sick. Bring them to God, that He might heal them, and so continue the work of Christ.

June 21   *Deuteronomy 19, Proverbs 9, Acts 3*

Command as God directs

Sometimes God will tell a person to speak a word of command. This is what happened when Peter and John met a crippled man at the Beautiful Gate of the temple in Jerusalem. He was begging for money, and Peter said to him, *"'Silver and gold have I none, but what I have I give you. In the name of Jesus Christ of Nazareth, rise up and walk!' And taking him by the right hand, he lifted him up, and immediately his feet and ankle-bones received strength"* (Acts 3:6,7). Immediately after Peter had commanded him to walk and lifted him to his feet, the man was healed. If God is telling you to speak a word of command, you will know. Obey, and you will see the works of God. Command as God directs.

June 22   *Deuteronomy 20, Proverbs 10, Acts 4*

Love your enemies

Whatever we do, none of us can entirely avoid having enemies in this life. Even Christ, the perfect man, had enemies who eventually killed Him. In his letter to the church at Rome, Paul draws from the book of Proverbs in advising his readers how to respond to their enemies. He writes, *"If your enemy is hungry, feed him; If he is thirsty, give him a drink; for in so doing you will heap coals of fire on his head"* (Romans 12:20). When we love our enemies, God works through our love to convict them of sin. There is no force greater than this when it comes to overcoming evil. Think of your enemies now, and ask God to show you how to love them. Release the power of conviction, and overcome evil with good.

June 23   *Deuteronomy 21, Proverbs 11, Acts 5*

Make generosity a habit

The book of Proverbs teaches that the path to godly prosperity is one of generosity: *"There is one who scatters, yet increases more; and there is one who withholds more than is right, but it leads to poverty. The generous soul will be made rich"* *(Proverbs 11:24,25)*. Generosity is a state of heart. It is those who earnestly seek to do good who find favour from God. Pray today, *"God create in me a generous heart, and help me not to miss any opportunity to give!"* Through practice, generosity can become a habit. Why not stop now and identify three specific ways in which you can be generous to others today? Plan these into your day. Practice generosity daily until it becomes automatic. Make generosity a habit!

June 24   *Deuteronomy 22, Proverbs 12, Acts 6*

Lift up your brother

The Law of Moses states, *"You shall not see your brother's donkey or his ox fall down along the road, and hide yourself from them: you shall surely help him lift them up again"* *(Deuteronomy 22:4)*. The animal represents their livelihood and well being. If we care, we will act to protect our neighbour, their property, and business. Jesus extended the commandment to love our neighbour, saying that we should even love our enemy (Matthew 5:44). How often have you been in difficulty and hoped that someone might help you get back on your feet again? In such situations there is no guarantee that anyone will come to your aid, which is why assistance of this kind can have such a powerful effect. Who can you lift up today?

June 25   *Deuteronomy 23, Proverbs 13, Acts 7*

Give a good measure

Never be stingy when you give. If you are not sure how much to give, it is better to give a bit more than a bit less. God loves cheerful givers, and rewards those who give a good measure. Jesus said, *"Give and it will be given to you: good measure, pressed down, shaken together, and running over will be put into your bosom. For with the same measure that you use, it will be measured back to you"* (Luke 6:38). What is a good measure? It is the measure God tells you to give. Happily give that, and in due season you will receive a good measure back. Take every opportunity to give in this way, and keep on giving what you can, in fat times and lean. It is not the amount, but the heart that matters. Give a good measure today!

June 26   *Deuteronomy 24, Proverbs 14, Acts 8*

Practice true religion

"When you reap your harvest in your field, and forget a sheaf in the field, you shall not go back to get it; it shall be for the stranger, the fatherless, and the widow, that the Lord your God may bless you in all the work of your hands" (Deuteronomy 24:19). God feels very strongly about the care of the vulnerable. Caring starts in the heart. Jesus was moved with compassion towards the suffering. We too should allow our hearts to be stirred. When we do, we are propelled towards others by the Love that moves the stars. We become God's ambassadors of healing, faithfully doing what we can. *"Pure and undefiled religion before God and the Father is this: to visit orphans and widows in their trouble"* (James 1:27).

June 27　　　　　　　　*Deuteronomy 25, Proverbs 15, Acts 9*

Accept His love

It has been said of human love that *"Love is blind"*. One person may think so highly of another that faults or failings are overlooked. If human love can be deep, God's love is deeper. If human love is strong, God's love is stronger. If human love is intense, God's love is more so. If human love transforms, God's love does so more! And yet, at the same time, God sees all. Despite knowing all about us, the good and the bad, His love remains constant. Nothing can shake it. If someone knows the truth about you, and loves you as much as ever, you have a true friend. God loves like this, with a love that is intensely passionate, yet absolutely objective. Such love makes the ultimate sacrifice, that we may be friends forever.

June 28　　　　　　　　*Deuteronomy 26, Proverbs 16, Acts 10*

Put God before tradition

In the early days of the Christian church, God showed Peter in a vision that salvation was as much for the Gentile as for the Jew. Immediately after, men came to Peter, inviting him to the home of Cornelius, a Roman centurion. God had told Cornelius that Peter had a message for him from God. Had Peter followed his traditions that day, he would neither have gone to the house, nor been open to what God was about to do. Tradition told him not to keep company with foreigners, but God said he, *"Should not call any man common or unclean" (Acts 10:28)*. So Peter went, and Cornelius and his household believed and were all filled with the Holy Spirit (Acts 10:44). Some conventions may be good, but obedience is best!

June 29   *Deuteronomy 27, Proverbs 17, Acts 11*

Smile!

A smile can say more than a thousand words. Make no effort to smile and you rob the world of joy. Smiles warm the heart and refresh the spirit. As Solomon says, *"A merry heart does good, like medicine, but a broken spirit dries the bones" (Proverbs 17:22)*. How many more smiles would we see if people knew their power? Smiles are more influential than many suppose. Sincere smiles send a positive message to others, encouraging dialogue and building relationships. Smiles make people relax. They lower anxiety and create a climate in which people can come together and do their best work. There is little as simple yet as powerful as a smile. Make a conscious decision to smile today, and note the difference it makes!

June 30   *Deuteronomy 28, Proverbs 18, Acts 12*

Choose true friends

The Bible says that, *"There is a friend who sticks closer than a brother" (Pr.18:24)*. Watch out for those who stand with you when things are tough, who stick with you through problems and difficulties. These are the kind of people to make your closest friends. Choose as your friends those whose hearts are towards you, whose actions show that they truly love and accept you. You may be surprised at who stands with you and who deserts you when things are tough. Beware of those who flatter you, but inwardly their hearts are far from you. Love them, but do not make them your friends or they may turn and rend you (Matthew 7:6). Keep from such, and build with those who prove worthy of your friendship.

July

July 1   *Deuteronomy 29, Proverbs 19, Acts 13*

Develop an understanding heart

Towards the end of Deuteronomy are found some sad words, spoken by Moses to the children of Israel. After reminding them of the great miracles that God performed when He delivered them from slavery in Egypt, he says, *"Yet the Lord has not given you a heart to perceive and eyes to see and ears to hear, to this very day" (Deuteronomy 29:4)*. God longs to give us such a heart, but He will never give us knowledge that we cannot be trusted with. Despite all they had seen and known of God, this people did not follow Him wholeheartedly. Had they done so, their wisdom and understanding would have been very great indeed. As we surrender all to God, and follow Him each day, He will surely give us that heart.

July 2   *Deuteronomy 30, Proverbs 20, Acts 14*

Use your spiritual senses

God has put a light in you, and that light is your spirit. In Proverbs we read that, *"The spirit of a man is the lamp of the Lord, searching all the inner depths of his heart" (Proverbs 20:27)*. The human spirit is a constant means of illumination and insight, but spiritual awareness must be cultivated. Practice listening to the promptings of your spirit and you will become increasingly sensitive to God's guidance. The writer of Hebrews refers to, *"Those who by reason of use have their senses trained to discern both good and evil" (Hebrews 4:14)*. Your spiritual senses will only develop as you use them. Why live in the dark when you can turn on the light? Listen to your spirit today, and receive all the wisdom you need.

July 3   *Deuteronomy 31, Proverbs 21, Acts 15*

Execute your plans with diligence

It is important not only that our plans are inspired by Heaven, but that they are faithfully followed on earth. Solomon says, *"The plans of the diligent lead surely to plenty, but those of everyone who is hasty, surely to poverty" (Proverbs 21:5).* Once we have received our orders from Heaven, we may be tempted to take things into our own hands, and do it our way. This can never lead to God's best, and may even jeopardise the heavenly mission. God's work must be done in God's way, and when it is, eternal success always follows. Having heard from Heaven let Heaven guide you in the execution of the plan. Start each day with a prayer that God will show you what to do to fulfil your mission that day.

July 4   *Deuteronomy 32, Proverbs 22, Acts 16*

Be in the Spirit

John says he, *"Was in the Spirit on the Lord's Day" (Revelation 1:10).* It might be thought that this was a mystical state reserved for spiritual giants, but nothing could be further from the truth. Yes, it was a remarkable revelation that he received, but being 'in the Spirit' was the easiest thing for John to do. We choose our interests, and can become engaged or enthralled by whatever we like. People do not find it hard to be captivated by what they enjoy. They get lost in their favourite television programme, they become absorbed in their hobby, or they become so focused on watching a game that they are oblivious to everything else. John simply got caught up in the Spirit. What happened next was God!

July 5   *Deuteronomy 33, Proverbs 23, Acts 17*

Take care what you tell yourself

Events clearly influence how we feel. If someone is pleasant to me, I may feel happy. If they are unpleasant I might feel unhappy. However, feelings cannot be explained simply in terms of the events we have experienced. There is another influence, and that is how we think about those events. Solomon says, *"As he thinks in his heart, so is he"* (Proverbs 23:7). If someone frowns at me and I think, *"He's concentrating on what I'm saying,"* I may feel respected. If I think, *"He's angry with me,"* I may feel angry too! If I think, *"He's looks tired and stressed,"* I may feel sorry for him. The same event can elicit different feelings, depending on how we think about it. Take care how you interpret events today.

July 6   *Deuteronomy 34, Proverbs 24, Acts 18*

Learn from what you see

King Solomon, a keen observer of life, once reflected on having walked past the field of a lazy man and seen it, *"All overgrown with thorns"* (Proverbs 24:30-34). Like other observant people before and after him, he found lessons and insights wherever he cast his gaze. We too can become wise by looking more carefully at the world around us. Take a closer look at your world today. Consider carefully what is around you, and learn the lessons it teaches. If you look carefully, you will see much that is helpful to you. Many opportunities are missed because people do not stop to look. Open your eyes, and see what you need to see. What can you learn from the school of life today?

July 7   *Joshua 1, Proverbs 25, Acts 19*

Be strong

When God called Joshua to his work, He said to him, *"Be strong and of good courage" (Joshua 1:6)*. All of us need strength and courage to do what God has called us to do. As you discover more of your heavenly calling, determine to pursue it with all the strength and courage you can find. In order to complete your life's work, you will need to overcome various obstacles that you will face along the way. These can all be overcome by drawing strength from God, and by courageously doing what He tells you to do. Do not flinch from that path. It is not the easiest path, but it is the greatest path. So *"Strengthen the weak hands, and make firm the feeble knees" (Isaiah 35:3)*. Be strong and courageous today.

July 8   *Joshua 2, Proverbs 26, Acts 20*

Put your trust in Him

There is no greater choice you will ever have to make than that of who or what to trust with your life. Rely on yourself alone and you will always be confined by your limited human resources, restricted by your human nature. Your life will be mundane, you will never transcend the limits of your humanity, and you will spend eternity apart from God. But choose to trust in Him, and you access unlimited and eternal resources, your corrupted human nature is transformed into His Divine nature, you can fulfil your life's true work, and you will spend eternity in Heaven. Faith is an open door through which all we need is supplied (Philippians 4:19). Let your choice be to trust God and follow Him today.

July 9   *Joshua 3, Proverbs 27, Acts 21*

Choose your heavenly job

We cannot always choose the paid work we would like to do in life, but we can choose to do the work God has called us to. It is so important that you do on earth what you have been put here to do by God. Paul writes that we have been created, *"For good works, which God prepared beforehand that we should walk in them" (Ephesians 2:10)*. God has given each person a definite purpose in life. Do you know what yours is? Listen to Him daily, and He will not only show you your calling, but also what to do to follow it. The key is to listen and obey. Some may oppose your work from God, but no one can stop you committing to His call in your heart. You have a unique calling. Whatever your situation, choose to do that job today.

July 10   *Joshua 4, Proverbs 28, Acts 22*

Choose true happiness

True happiness is friendship with God. *"Happy are the people whose God is the Lord" (Psalm 144:15b)*. God loves people and does everything He can to be friends with each one. Make Him your friend, and His Spirit will revive your own. Many things can make you happy for a moment, but only God can make you happy for eternity. Reject happiness with Him, and there is no alternative happy future. As C S Lewis said, *"God cannot give us happiness apart from Himself. It simply does not exist!"* If you desire greater happiness, spend more time with your Friend, the Source of true happiness. His word will lift you up. *"Happy is the man who is always reverent, but he who hardens his heart will fall into calamity" (Proverbs 28:14)*.

July 11   *Joshua 5, Proverbs 29, Acts 23*

Make your plans

Solomon says, *"A man's heart plans his way, but the Lord directs his steps" (Proverbs 16:9)*. It is good to plan. People who fail to plan often achieve less, and are in danger of being driven by every wind that blows. A vision or plan provides direction and purpose. You know where you are going, so you can be focused. Without a vision, energy is dissipated, resources are wasted, valuable time is lost, and instead of peace and security, there is anarchy and chaos. Solomon puts it best: *"Where there is no prophetic vision, the people cast off restraint" (Proverbs 29:18)*. You need a plan, not just any plan, but the plan God has for you. Seek Him and He will progressively reveal that great plan to you. Pray and make your plan today.

July 12   *Joshua 6, Proverbs 30, Acts 24*

Tune in to the 'still small voice'

There is far more to you than just your mind and body. God is a spirit (John 4:24), and as a person made in His image, you also are a spirit. The human spirit is formed by God (Zechariah 12:1) and part of our make-up from conception. However, the spirit is dead to God, and only comes alive through the experience of salvation. Jesus said that unless we experience spiritual rebirth we will neither see, nor enter God's kingdom (John 3:3-5). Through salvation the spirit is made new (Ezekiel 11:19; Romans 7:6) and starts to show us truth from heaven. But are we listening? Some suppress the spirit, but others listen. They tune in to the 'still small voice', and in following the spirit they are like the wind.

July 13   *Joshua 7, Proverbs 31, Acts 25*

Get up!

Following military defeat at Ai, Joshua was deeply upset and turned to God, asking Him why He was leading them to their death. In his distress, he started to think inaccurately about things and to draw the wrong conclusions. He was even regretting having set out on the mission. Unchallenged, these wrong thoughts might have robbed him and his people of a great deal. Therefore God spoke strongly to him saying, *"Get up! Why do you lie thus on your face?" (Joshua 7:10)*. When you experience disappointment and failure, grieve and face the facts, but do not lie down in the face of defeat. Rise up and go to God! Not only will He give you an accurate picture, He will show you what to do next. Get up.

July 14   *Joshua 8, Ecclesiastes 1, Acts 26*

Share your revelation

For centuries God has been building His church on the rock of revelation and faith (Matthew 16:18). Through the witness of those who respond to His call, His word reaches those who need to hear it. These are the pioneers of the gospel who go out carrying the revelation that Christ is the promised Son of God, the Saviour of the world. By their obedience, the word of faith goes to the nations and on that foundation God builds His church. Its walls rise tall and strong, and the gates of hell cannot stand against it. If we are Christ's, it is to this company that we belong. With whom could you share a revelation from God that would draw them nearer to Him? Share your revelation, and build something strong today.

July 15   *Joshua 9, Ecclesiastes 2, Acts 27*

Ask counsel of the Lord

As Joshua led his people into the Promised Land, there was a time when he was tricked by some of the indigenous people. The Bible records that the reason they fell for it was because, *"They did not ask counsel of the Lord" (Joshua 9:14)*. How important it is that we seek the Lord on all matters. Some laugh at this idea, but their smiles soon disappear when they are taken in. Unless we consistently seek the counsel of the Lord, we will easily be fooled by appearances, for things are not always as they seem. Appearances can be deceptive. By all means use your senses, your human experience, and your judgement, but do not be so foolish to rely on these alone. Check out the counsel of the Lord!

July 16   *Joshua 10, Ecclesiastes 3, Acts 28*

Hear a good word from God

When Paul says: *"Be anxious for nothing" (Philippians 4:6)*, he is offering us an alternative to unhelpful anxiety. Unhealthy anxiety sees threats, but not from Heaven's viewpoint. Solomon writes, *"Anxiety in the heart of man causes depression, but a good word makes it glad" (Proverbs 12:25)*. When we are worried, we need a 'good word' that will encourage us and give us strength to go on. That is exactly the word of faith that God gives us when we turn to Him with our worries. *"Let your requests be made known to God, and the peace of God, which surpasses all understanding, will guard your hearts and minds through Christ Jesus" (Philippians 4:6,7)*. Take your worries to God today and believe the answer He gives.

July 17   *Joshua 11, Ecclesiastes 4, Romans 1*

Defeat the Lie of lies

The apostle Paul describes those who, *"Exchanged the truth of God for the lie, and worshipped and served the creature rather than the Creator" (Romans 1:25).* What is this lie of which Paul speaks? This is the lie that inspired the rebellion of Lucifer in Heaven, the lie that robbed humanity of Eden, and the lie that has devastated and destroyed the lives of men and women through every century to this day. There is no more toxic idea than the belief that one will be better off acting independently of God. We must resist this lie above all others. Every day you will be tempted to do things your way rather than God's. The answer is simple: turn back to God each day, trust Him, and do things His way. Defeat the Lie of lies.

July 18   *Joshua 12, Ecclesiastes 5, Romans 2*

Escape the prison of self-deception

Self-deception is the most dangerous deception of all. Once we have deceived ourselves, we no longer see the truth in that area. Being convinced, we remain blind, for conviction validates our chosen lie. The self-deceived cannot rescue themselves. They will only escape from the prison of delusion if another reveals the truth to them in a way that cannot be denied. This will happen on the day of judgement. Paul writes of, *"A day when God shall judge the secrets of men by Jesus Christ" (Romans 2:16).* Nothing will remain hidden on that day. But we do not have to wait until then. Ask God to show you where you have deceived yourself, and He will. Why wait, when you can enjoy the freedom of truth now?

July 19 *Joshua 13, Ecclesiastes 6, Romans 3*

Fire the arrow of your life

When we take a closer look at our goals, we may find that some need working on. For example, if we identify goals that are a poor expression of our principles or our calling, then we will want to change them. If we see long term goals that are unachievable, we will want to modify them so that they can be reached. If we spot short term goals that are too ambitious, we will want to reduce them to bite-sized chunks. Goal management is an important part of life. When goals are prayerfully selected and faithfully followed under the direction of the Holy Spirit, great good can be achieved. Take a moment today to review and sharpen your goals. Your life is like an arrow. Take aim before you fire.

July 20 *Joshua 14, Ecclesiastes 7, Romans 4*

Get your goals from God

If you are to reach your goals, they must be achievable. An achievable goal is one you can reasonably expect to reach given the resources available to you. Resources are one of the greatest contributory factors to success. The more relevant resources you can employ in the service of your aims, the more you may achieve. Without God, whatever earthly resources you have are finite and limited, but with God, you have access to the unlimited and infinite resources of eternity. For the Christian, an achievable goal is any goal that God has given. If God says it, however impossible it may seem, it *can* be done. As Wesley put it, *"Faith, the mighty promise sees, laughs at impossibilities, and says 'It will be done!'"*

July 21   *Joshua 15, Ecclesiastes 8, Romans 5*

Go for the goal above all goals

Of all the goals you might choose, one in particular will both advance God's work and make you whole. There is no other goal like it. This goal is unique in its simplicity and power. This was the goal of the heroes of Scripture and the great saints of history. This is the one goal above all that defeats the devil. Faithfulness to this goal would have prevented the Fall. Commitment to this goal will bring the greatest rewards in eternity. This goal is so simple and so easy that it may be followed by adult or child. What is this goal? It is the goal of hearing and obeying God. Make it your goal in all things to listen to God and follow His directions. Write a reminder to do this and place it where you will see it, lest you forget.

July 22   *Joshua 16, Ecclesiastes 9, Romans 6*

Know how you feel

The capacity to experience emotion is one of the qualities that define our humanity. God made us capable of experiencing a wealth of emotions, too great to fully measure. If we analysed all literature for every emotional expression, we would create a vast database, but because of language limitations, even this would fail to describe the full riches of emotional experience. Such emotional richness has the potential to benefit us greatly, but this potential often remains unrealised, largely because we have not adequately developed our ability to handle feelings. Emotions need to be acknowledged and well managed if they are going to play a helpful role in your life. What emotions can you identify in yourself today?

July 23   *Joshua 17, Ecclesiastes 10, Romans 7*

Learn from your emotions

In the Psalms, King David often talks about his feelings. Facing how we feel is the first step towards good emotional management. Emotions are helpful indicators. If acknowledged and understood, they can show us key aspects of ourselves that we might not otherwise see. Emotions reflect how we see things, alerting us to helpful or unhelpful attitudes and perceptions. When we see the value of learning from feelings, we will give them due attention. Whenever you become aware of a feeling, ask yourself what thoughts might be generating that emotion. Keep practicing this, until you become skilful in understanding your emotions. Learn to face your feelings and understand why you feel as you do.

July 24   *Joshua 18, Ecclesiastes 11, Romans 8*

Be led by The Spirit

Paul writes, *"For as many as are led by the Spirit of God, these are sons of God" (Romans 8:14)*. As a son or daughter of God, it is your birthright to be led by the Spirit moment by moment. Even when you think you know the way, check it out with God. He can see things you cannot see, and will guide you by the best route. Submit all your plans and actions to Him. Only the Spirit of God can guide you in your calling from God. Walk by the light of the Spirit and He will show you the path to take, prompting you to act as you should, and bringing you to the successful conclusion of your life and work. There may be many storms, but under His care you will weather them all. Be led by the Spirit, today and every day.

July 25   *Joshua 19, Ecclesiastes 12, Romans 9*

Accept God's mercy

Saint Paul describes the inability of humanity to ensure their eternal well-being through self effort. He says, *"So then it is not of him who wills, nor of him who runs, but of God who shows mercy" (Romans 9:16).* No human will has the power to obtain its own salvation. No human act is effective enough to achieve eternal life apart from God. It is only by God's mercy that we are assured of eternal life. Through the sacrifice of Christ, who paid the penalty for our sin, God has done what we could never do, opening the way for us to be friends with Him forever. If we believe this and trust in Him, we will live. The way to righteousness is by faith (v.30). Rejoice today that you are saved by grace, and grace alone!

July 26   *Joshua 20, Song of Songs 1, Romans 10*

Keep your spiritual eyes open

Faith is spiritual sight. When we consciously look to God, our faith grows in relation to everything He shows us. This is a biblical truth. When Paul says that, *"We walk by faith, not by sight" (2 Corinthians 5:7),* he is referring to the fact that those who walk with God have another way of seeing things. They do not just see the visible physical realm, but they see by revelation of the Holy Spirit. They see things that God shows them, things they would never see by physical sense alone. As they look to God and listen to Him, faith grows, for *"Faith comes by hearing, and hearing by the Word of God" (Romans 10:17).* Keep your spiritual eyes open as you walk through each day. If you see it in your spirit, you will believe it.

July 27   *Joshua 21, Song of Songs 2, Romans 11*

Take your worries to the King

What do you do with your cares and woe? Some people drown them in alcohol, some bury them in the unconscious to silence their screams, some take them to the marriage altar to soften them with love, some take them to work to answer them with achievement, some take them to the therapist, but the best place of all to take our worries is to God. Peter says, *"Humble yourselves under the mighty hand of God, that He may exalt you in due time, casting all your care upon Him, for He cares for you" (1 Peter 5:6,7)*. Take them to God. Take them all and take them now. Do not hold anything back. Give it all to God, every worry, every fear, every anxiety. Cast the lot on Him, and having cast, wait for His word to you.

July 28   *Joshua 22, Song of Songs 3, Romans 12*

Take careful heed

What do you take the most care over? When Joshua released the tribe of Reuben, the tribe of Gad, and half the tribe of Manasseh, to go to their lands, he said to them, *"Take careful heed to do the commandment and the law which Moses the servant of the Lord commanded you, to love the Lord your God, to walk in all His ways, to keep His commandments, to hold fast to Him, and to serve Him with all your heart and with all your soul" (Joshua 22:5)*. Joshua urges his people to walk closely with God, the great key to living. He knew that unless people are careful to follow this path, they can be easily deceived by sin, and robbed. So he reminded them. Remind yourself to seek God daily and walk closely with Him, your number one concern.

July 29   *Joshua 23, Song of Songs 4, Romans 13*

Use fresh oil

"But my horn You have exalted like a wild ox; I have been anointed with fresh oil" (Psalm 92:10). Whether we are frying food or running a car, we know that there comes a time when the oil needs to be changed, a point where we need fresh oil. Oil is a biblical symbol of the Holy Spirit. God knows that we need a fresh anointing of the Spirit every day. As we walk with Him from day to day, He fills us anew and anoints us afresh with His Holy Spirit. The result is that we are transformed and empowered. Don't rely on old oil. It is no use for today. As you submit to Him each morning, God will anoint you for the work of that day. You will receive *all* the grace you need. Thank God for fresh oil.

July 30   *Joshua 24, Song of Songs 5, Romans 14*

Use your influence for good

Joshua says to God's people, *"And if it seems evil to you to serve the Lord, Choose for yourselves this day whom you will serve ... But as for me and my house, we will serve the Lord" (Joshua 24:15).* God will not usurp the will. He will do everything He possibly can to help us make the right choices, but He will no more force the unrighteous to enter Heaven, than He will force the righteous out of it! We choose, and God ratifies the choice we have made, even to the choice of our eternal destiny. God has given us the power to choose, and He will honour the choices that we make. You and I can influence the choices people make. So let us choose what is good, and seize every opportunity to help others choose what is good, today!

July 31   *Judges 1, Song of Songs 6, Romans 15*

Abound in hope!

Any loss can sadden you, but lose something you value greatly, with no hope of restoring it, and you may move from sadness to depression. When the light of hope goes out, it is invariably replaced by the darkness of despair. Hope is the antidote to reactive depression. Therefore you must keep hope alive. When hopes die that are not of God, change your thinking so that it agrees with His. But when godly hopes are dashed, go to God and hear His word on it. That word will bring faith and restore hope. So shall, *"The God of hope fill you with all joy and peace in believing, that you may abound in hope by the power of the Holy Spirit" (Romans 15:13)*. When events get you down, let God lift you up. Abound in hope today.

AUGUST

August 1   *Judges 2, Song of Songs 7, Romans 16*

Beware of hypocrites

Sadly, some use Christianity as a cloak to conceal their true plans and purposes. Paul describes such people in his letter to the church at Rome, and instructs his readers to avoid them: *"For those who are such do not serve our Lord Jesus Christ, but their own belly, and by smooth words and flattering speech deceive the hearts of the simple" (Romans 16:18)*. The wise recognise that there will be deception in the church until Christ returns. Like the Jews of Berea, who took time to check out the preaching of Paul and Silas, they test everything against the witness of the Holy Spirit and the word of God (Acts 17:11). God will show you who's who in the church, but you must listen to Him. It is the only way to avoid being taken in.

August 2   *Judges 3, Song of Songs 8, 1 Corinthians 1*

Recognise your frustrations

When needs, desires, purposes, or goals are frustrated, it is natural for us to feel some degree of anger. Because such frustrations are common, the possibility of anger will never be far away, and anger management becomes a prerequisite for successful living. Badly managed, anger can have destructive consequences, damaging lives (Proverbs 29:22). Some are victims of their own anger, whilst others are victims of somebody else's anger. Well managed, anger can be a force for personal growth and positive social change. Identifying our anger and understanding its causes are the foundations of effective anger management. When you are next angry, ask yourself, "What demand or goal is being frustrated here?"

August 3 *Judges 4, Isaiah 1, 1 Corinthians 2*

Make Jesus your focus

In his first letter to the church at Corinth, Paul reminds them of his visit. He says, *"And I brethren, when I came to you, did not come with excellence of speech or of wisdom declaring to you the testimony of God. For I determined not to know anything among you except Jesus Christ and Him crucified" (1 Corinthians 2:2)*. He modelled to them the one focus necessary, the one path to life – Jesus only! If we will follow his example, God will move in power (v.4), the way of the Spirit will open to us (v.12), and we will know the mind of Christ (v.16). There is no greater way than this, the way of Christ Himself. Jesus said, *"You believe in God, believe also in Me ... I am the way, the truth, and the life. No man comes to the Father except through Me" (John 14:1,6)*.

August 4 *Judges 5, Isaiah 2, 1 Corinthians 3*

Build with Heaven's materials

Paul challenges us to be careful what we build in this life. He says, *"No other foundation can anyone lay than that which is laid, which is Jesus Christ. Now if anyone builds on this foundation with gold, silver, precious stones, wood, hay, straw, each one's work will become clear; for the Day will declare it ... If anyone's work which he has built on it endures, he will receive a reward" (1 Corinthians 3:11-14)*. Look beyond this life when you decide what to do. Ask yourself, *"What is this worth in Heaven's economy?"* Some things that are esteemed of little value on earth, have great value in Heaven, whilst others that are highly regarded here, are of small value in God's sight. So reject the worthless, and build with gold, silver, and precious stones today.

August 5   *Judges 6, Isaiah 3, 1 Corinthians 4*

Make a rapid response

Christ clearly taught the reality of Satan, and summarised his evil manifesto, saying, *"The thief does not come except to steal, and to kill, and to destroy" (John 10:10).* The devil pursues this policy using a variety of stratagems, including temptations intended to distort our thinking, attacks on our spirit that may include confrontation or oppression, and even physical assaults on the body that my bring disease, lethargy, or stress. The key is to submit to God and stay close to Him. He will give us discernment, and show us what to do when we are under spiritual attack. James says, *"Resist the devil and he will flee from you" (James 3:7).* When 'under fire' we should make a rapid response, submitting to God, and resisting the devil.

August 6   *Judges 7, Isaiah 4, 1 Corinthians 5*

Win by obedience

Gideon's victory, described in Judges 7, teaches an important lesson in spiritual obedience. When God called him to lead an army against the invaders who plundered and oppressed his nation, Gideon was obedient and gathered his forces for battle. Although his army of thirty two thousand was smaller than that of the enemy, God told him it was too large and made him cut it by two thirds. Then God said it was still too big and made him cut it more, until Gideon was left with three hundred men. He now appeared to face certain defeat, but the Great Commander was directing him with the most perfect strategy. The way to win your battles is not primarily by might or cunning plans, but by the counsel of the Lord.

August 7　　　　　　　　　*Judges 8, Isaiah 5, 1 Corinthians 6*

Hear the cry of guilt

Guilt feelings alert us to the fact that we have done something we believe we should not have done, or omitted to do something we believe we should have done. They are great helpers, for their timely alerts enable us to live by our deeply held principles. How many evil schemes have died unborn, how many dark impulses have been frustrated, and how many injuries have been avoided, because the cry of guilt was heeded? When you feel guilty, stop and listen to your guilt. What does it tell you? If it is true guilt, go to God, and find the right way of doing things. If it is false guilt, change your thinking, and kill the feeling. Either way, you will be glad you listened when the cry of guilt sounded in your soul.

August 8　　　　　　　　　*Judges 9, Isaiah 6, 1 Corinthians 7*

Be honest about your guilt

The fact of guilt and the feeling of guilt should go together. If you *are* guilty, it is appropriate to *feel* guilty. But there are times when being guilty and feeling guilty can get separated. For example, the guilty often deny their sins and bury their guilt feelings. This is a dangerous place to be, as they develop a false confidence built on self deception. Jesus condemned the Scribes and Pharisees for doing this, saying, *"Fill up, then, the measure of your fathers' guilt" (Matthew 23:32)*. They pretended they were righteous, but Christ said that inside they were, *"Full of extortion and unrighteousness ...dead men's bones and all uncleanness ...hypocrisy and lawlessness" (vv.25,27+28)*. Confess your sin, and turn from it today.

August 9 *Judges 10, Isaiah 7, 1 Corinthians 8*

Test your idols

In the book of Judges, God challenges His people over their idolatry, saying, *"Go and cry out to the gods which you have chosen; let them deliver you in your time of distress"* (Judges 10:14). Some people will trust anything rather than God. Their idols are not restricted to gods of wood and stone, but extend to a great range of dependencies, a vast pantheon of 'gods'. Ability, intelligence, wealth, influence, work, friends, family, relationships, or any other thing, may be elevated to the place that only God can fill. So God says to put these idols to the test, and when we do, we soon find that, being finite, they are lousy gods. Examine yourself today to ensure that nothing has taken His place in your life. There is no God like the Lord.

August 10 *Judges 11, Isaiah 8, 1 Corinthians 9*

Face your shame now

Whenever you face exposure of yourself in areas you do not feel right or good about, you become a candidate for shame. In life, much sin remains hidden. We typically hide from others things we are ashamed of, and even deny such things to ourselves, preferring not to see them. Sometimes people try to avoid shame by preserving the appearance of correctness. Others may be fooled, but not God. A day is coming when the secrets of every heart will be revealed. Great will be the shame of many on that day, when Light exposes every sin. There will be nowhere to run and hide. But for those who face their sin now in repentance to God, shame is swallowed up by confidence. Face your shame today, and wave it goodbye.

August 11   *Judges 12, Isaiah 9, 1 Corinthians 10*

Be ambitious for God

"Whether you eat or drink, or whatever you do, do all to the glory of God" (1 Corinthians 10:31). Ambition is a powerful force, driving activity in pursuit of personal goals. What are your ambitions? The foolish seek fame and glory for themselves, as if it was something lasting, but the wise see that folly and seek instead the glory of God. Whose glory are you seeking? Choose your own glory and you are eternally bankrupt. Choose the glory of God and you enjoy rewards that last forever. When we yield our lives to Him, giving Him His rightful throne in our hearts, loving Him and submitting to His loving authority, ambitious to do His will, the glory will be His and His alone!

August 12   *Judges 13, Isaiah 10, 1 Corinthians 11*

Come to the light

Some sin without feeling guilty, whilst others feel guilty without having sinned. Such is the power of the mind, that it can paint black white and white black. Unaware of this power, we risk falling into the trap of false righteousness or the trap of false guilt. The former is the state of the guilty that see themselves as innocent. The latter is the condition of the righteous that see themselves condemned. How is your moral sight? Unable to see sin clearly, you will surely fall. There is only one place to stand from which you can get a clear view of sin, and that is with God. James says, *"Draw near to God, and He will draw near to you" (James 4:8).* Listen to Him, and He will convict you clearly of both sin and righteousness.

August 13 *Judges 14, Isaiah 11, 1 Corinthians 12*

Expect the unexpected

God does not always work in the way we expect. When the young Samson fell in love with a Philistine woman, against the customs of his people, his mother tried to dissuade him, but, *"His father and mother did not know that it was of the Lord"* *(Judges 14:4)*. God had a plan, and to accomplish it He worked in a way that no one expected. The stories of Scripture and history both attest to the unexpectedness of God. If we walk closely with Him, His ways will not take us by surprise, but if we live merely according to what we think He will do, however well informed by Biblical or theological study, we may fail to recognise God at work. Walk with Him, and move in the unexpected.

August 14 *Judges 15, Isaiah 12, 1 Corinthians 13*

Cultivate the greatest fruit

Of all the fruit of the Holy Spirit's presence in our lives, there is none greater than love. If we are going to develop the character of God, we should earnestly desire this greatest gift. Ask God for more love, and it will be given you. Here is a prayer to pray from the heart: *Give me love Lord, that I am patient and kind, that I do not envy, that I do not boast, and that I am not arrogant. Give me love Lord, that I am not rude, that I am not self-seeking, that I am not easily angered, and that I think no evil. Give me love Lord that I do not rejoice at wrong but rejoice in the truth. Give me love Lord, that I bear all things, that I always believe, that I always hope, and that I always persevere. Thank you that love never fails! In Jesus' name. Amen.*

August 15   *Judges 16, Isaiah 13, 1 Corinthians 14*

Beware of prolonged stress

Under high levels of sustained pressure people often 'break down' one way or another. This is what happened to Samson, a man of great strength and intellect. He was playing a game with Delilah, teasing her over the secret of his strength. He knew that the Philistines were out to kill him, and he was confident that he could outwit and outfight his enemies. Delilah however wore him down day after day, until he broke and told her his secret (Judges 16:16-21). His mistake cost him dear. At least three lessons can be learnt here: (1) do not put yourself under too much stress; (2) do not trust in your own strength and cleverness; and (3) do not play games with the devil! Learn from Samson and beat stress before it beats you!

August 16   *Judges 17, Isaiah 14, 1 Corinthians 15*

Expect a great future

Both those who live in Christ and those who die in Him have nothing to fear regarding eternity. A wonderful transformation will occur at Christ's return, in which our bodies will be made immortal and set free from all decay (1 Corinthians 15:51-54). This will happen, *"In a moment, in the twinkling of an eye,"* when the last trumpet sounds (v.52). *"For the Lord Himself will descend from heaven with a shout, with the voice of an archangel, and with the trumpet of God. And the dead in Christ will rise first. Then we who are alive and remain shall be caught up together with them in the clouds to meet the Lord in the air. And thus we shall always be with the Lord"* (1 Thessalonians 5:16,17). You have a great future in a perfect body.

August 17   *Judges 18, Isaiah 15, 1 Corinthians 16*

Believe in the Lord Jesus Christ

How do we experience spiritual rebirth? Just as physical birth is the product of physical union, spiritual birth is the fruit of spiritual union with God. Physical birth is from below, earthly. Spiritual birth is from above, heavenly. Flesh begets flesh. Spirit begets spirit. Physical birth enables us to experience earthly things, but spiritual birth enables us to see heavenly things. To be reborn of the Spirit is to be united with God. God has made this possible by removing the sin that prevented us being united with Him. He became human, took all our sin upon Himself, and broke its power at the cross. Because of this, whoever believes in Him is born again and has everlasting life. Put your faith in Him today.

August 18   *Judges 19, Isaiah 16, 2 Corinthians 1*

Devote your life to Heaven's business

God says, *"When you pass through the waters, I will be with you; and through the rivers, they shall not overflow you. When you walk through the fire, you shall not be burned"* (Isaiah 43:2). In strong poetic language He describes the deliverance of those who fear Him. God never promises freedom from suffering. Jesus would not have said, *"Do not fear those who kill the body"* (Matthew 10:28), if we were exempt from danger. Instead He says that while you are on Heaven's business you will have Heaven's bodyguards. God will deliver you until it is your time to leave and be with Christ. When trouble comes, *"We should not trust in ourselves, but in God who raises the dead"* (2 Corinthians 1:9). Devote your life to Heaven's business.

August 19   *Judges 20, Isaiah 17, 2 Corinthians 2*

Take action against depression

Depression involves hormonal changes resulting from our reaction to events, physiological problems, or spiritual influences. It is a cruel foe, whose weapons injure millions daily. Whether young or old, rich or poor, famous or unknown, none are exempt from possible attack. How should you fight this enemy? Firstly: recognise it. The sooner you see what is happening, the sooner you can take action. When you are down, be honest about it. Secondly: seek to find out why you are depressed. Ask God to help you discover the cause. Thirdly: take corrective action. Improve any negative thought patterns, and where depression is moderate to severe, seek medical advice. If you are down, take action today.

August 20   *Judges 21, Isaiah 18, 2 Corinthians 3*

Seek God's morality

The final verse in Judges describes the moral state of a nation that had turned from God: *"In those days there was no king in Israel; everyone did what was right in his own eyes" (Judges 21:25).* They followed their own morality, rather than God's. We each have a conscience, but until it is fully renewed by the Spirit, conscience is a fallible guide, being programmed by a range of influences, varying in accuracy. Follow conscience, and your actions may seem right to you, but they may not be right in God's sight. The only way to ensure you do what is *truly* right is to stay close to God and follow His moral guidance. Life presents us with difficult moral challenges, but if we seek God's moral direction, we will find it.

August 21   *Ruth 1, Isaiah 19, 2 Corinthians 4*

Make the greatest choice

The book of Ruth tells of how God can bring good out of grief. Following the death of her husband, Ruth chose to stay with her mother-in-law Naomi, rather than return to her own people. She said to Naomi, *"Where you go, I will go. Where you stay, I will stay. Your people shall be my people, and your God my God" (Ruth 1:16).* Her decision to trust in the Lord was the greatest decision she made in her life. For Ruth, this decision took her to Bethlehem, put her in a new marriage with Boaz, and gave her a son Obed, who was to be the grandfather of King David. Remember today that your choice to trust God and follow Him will have positive impact, not only during your life, but also after you have gone!

August 22   *Ruth 2, Isaiah 20, 2 Corinthians 5*

Walk by faith, not by sight

Paul says, *"We walk by faith, not by sight" (2 Corinthians 5:7).* Fail to grasp this and your healing ministry will die unborn. If you are more swayed by the sight of the sickness than you are established in the faith of God, you will not pray for the sick with vigour. But if you are moved more by what you believe than by what you see, you will get results. You may or may not see those results immediately. Perhaps the person will be wholly healed in an instant. Perhaps it will be obvious that a partial healing has taken place. But it is also possible that there will be no outward evidence of what God has just done. Whatever the visible outcome, faith 'sees' the invisible, and stands firm on what God has said. Walk by faith!

August 23   *Ruth 3, Isaiah 21, 2 Corinthians 6*

Finish your work from God for today

Knowing which tasks to prioritise is one of the greatest challenges we face in managing our time. Some things are clearly important or urgent, requiring our prompt attention, but not everything is so easy to rank. Some tasks that seem urgent may be better left for a while, whilst some seemingly insignificant actions may be more important than we think. How can you tell what is really important? Time management principles can take you so far, but to get your priorities right every time, you need to let God guide what you do, and the order you do it in. Be like Boaz, of whom it was said that he, *"Will not rest until he has finished the matter today"* (Ruth 3:18). The work to finish today is the work God gave you.

August 24   *Ruth 4, Isaiah 22, 2 Corinthians 7*

Steer your life for God

Experience and behaviour require self control, if life is to be fully lived. How we interpret our experience and how we act in response to those interpretations, profoundly influences our destiny. It is therefore of the utmost importance that we examine and understand both our perceptions and our responses. Only then can we take control of our direction in life. As Socrates says, the unexamined life is not worth living. It is like a ship without navigation that founders upon the rocks. Ensure you have firm hold of the helm today. Take your course from God and ask two basic questions: *"What am I saying to myself?"* and *"What am I doing?"* This way, you will learn to steer your life by Heaven's compass.

August 25   1 Samuel 1, Isaiah 23, 2 Corinthians 8

Pray for the sick

Following His resurrection and immediately before His ascension into Heaven, Christ commissioned every believer to go and pray for the sick. His simple statement, *"They will lay hands on the sick, and they will be well" (Mark 16:18)*, not only makes it clear that anyone can pray for the sick, but that people are going to get well. Contrary to what is sometimes thought, praying for the sick is not just for priests, pastors, or those with special gifts of healing. It is something for everyone. Even a child can do it. Who do you know that is sick? Pray for their complete recovery. You are not the Healer, but you can be the minister of healing. Pray for them in faith, commit them to God, and leave the rest to Him.

August 26   1 Samuel 2, Isaiah 24, 2 Corinthians 9

Give of your increase

Do not let your vision be limited by your current resources. Remember that God is the Supplier and Multiplier of your resources. Giving resources is the best way of growing resources. Paul compares giving to sowing seed with God. As we give cheerfully and bountifully out of the increase of our wealth, it will be multiplied back to us. He prays, *"He who supplies seed to the sower, and bread for eating, may He supply and multiply your seed, and increase the fruits of your righteousness" (2 Corinthians 9:10)*. Keep giving of your increase and you will grow and grow and grow! *"God is able to make all grace abound toward you, that in everything, always having all self-sufficiency, you may abound to every good work" (v.8)*.

August 27 1 Samuel 3, Isaiah 25, 2 Corinthians 10

Take up your builders tools

Sometimes an old building is extensively developed and modified, so that its architecture reflects different periods and styles. Our psychological defences tend to grow like this. The inner castle we build to protect ourselves reflects the many different defensive decisions we have made. What influences do you see when you study the architecture of your soul? If you are inquiring and honest, you will see a variety of these, some more helpful, others less so. Take an inventory of these 'styles'. Then take up your builders tools and go to work, *"Casting down arguments and every high thing that exalts itself against the knowledge of God, bringing every thought into captivity to the obedience of Christ"* (2 Corinthians 10:5).

August 28 1 Samuel 4, Isaiah 26, 2 Corinthians 11

Seek God early

The prophet Isaiah says, *"I will seek You early"* (Isaiah 26:9). He knew the importance of prompt spiritual action! How do we approach the daily business and challenges of life? Do we jump straight in and work, without consulting Heaven, or do we go straight to God in prayer on it, and let Him guide and prosper our work. Action is vital, but is it based on prayer? Our natural human tendency is to do it our way, but this can be changed through practice. If we consciously practice involving God early on in every decision we make, consulting Him will soon become an automatic response. We will soon see the benefits of early action, as God makes a way for us through all the seasons of life.

August 29   1 Samuel 5, Isaiah 27, 2 Corinthians 12

Build spiritual fitness

A marathon runner gradually builds up stamina by disciplined regular practice. As it is in the natural, so it is also in the spirit. Do not wait for a crisis before you pray. Pray now. Develop your spiritual muscles in the time of peace, so that you may be able to overcome in the day of adversity. Now is the time to build spiritual stamina, suppleness, and strength. If you will train your spirit, you will acquire the suppleness of the wind, the strength of faith, and the stamina of eternity. Make spiritual fitness training your first priority each day. *"Those who wait on the Lord shall renew their strength; they shall mount up with wings like eagles, they shall run and not be weary, they shall walk and not faint"* (Isaiah 40:31).

August 30   1 Samuel 6, Isaiah 28, 2 Corinthians 13

Have faith in God for healing

Although healing ministry can take many forms, there are recurring themes. One of the greatest of these is faith. Often when we pray for the sick, faith proves a vital ingredient. James says, *"The prayer of faith will cure the sick"* (James 5:15). Do not waste your time praying faithless prayers. Faith comes by hearing. It will come as you look to God, hear Him, and pray as He directs. Pray like this, and God's grace will work to bring His solutions, whatever they are. Keep praying, allowing faith to rise ever more strongly in your heart. Keep praying until you sense you have 'prayed it through'. God's power can flow through your prayer to change things, if you will pray God's way. Have faith in God for healing today.

August 31   *1 Samuel 7, Isaiah 29, Galatians 1*

See yourself as God sees you

God has dressed creation in many colours. The great richness and diversity of the natural world speaks of the Creator's love for all. God is not monotonous, but paints with every colour on His palette, mixing His colours with the greatest precision to create the most outstanding effects. If you were an artist, what portrait would you paint of yourself? Would you paint in bright colours or in sombre tones? True religion sets people free to paint with all the colours, as the Holy Spirit becomes their inspiration. Pick up your imaginary paintbrush now and create a beautiful painting in your mind that represents who you are in God. As you pass through the day, go back every now and then to view and enjoy that painting.

SEPTEMBER

September 1   *1 Samuel 8, Isaiah 30, Galatians 2*

Receive God's forgiveness

Those racked by guilt often feel trapped because they cannot go back and undo what they have done. Days can be filled with despair, and nights with the torment of memories and regrets. What do you do if the pain of guilt is so strong that you can hardly bear it? The first step is to bring your guilt to God. He promises that if we confess our sins, He will forgive us and cleanse us from all unrighteousness. The next step is to actually believe this. Unless you believe that you are forgiven, you will have no relief from the pain of guilt. Faith takes hold of forgiveness, feeding on it until the soul is filled with the grace of sin forgiven. You can receive God's forgiveness and find freedom from sin today.

September 2   *1 Samuel 9, Isaiah 31, Galatians 3*

Know what you need to know

When ancient Israel asked for a king, God showed the prophet Samuel whom He had chosen. *"Now the Lord had told Samuel in his ear the day before Saul came" (1 Samuel 9:15).* There are times when God directs with particular clarity, and this was one of them. It is not always like this. Sometimes the answers we seek are less clear, or come in ways we do not expect. When we go to Him for direction, we should do so with an open heart and mind. It is perfectly reasonable to seek answers to our questions, but when we listen for His reply we must take care that we come with an open mind. There are times when what we *want* to know may not be what we *need* to know. Let God guide you *His* way.

September 3　　　　　　　　1 Samuel 10, Isaiah 32, Galatians 4

Make God your King

There came a point in their history when ancient Israel rejected God's plan of government. He had established their nation as a theocracy, but many did not want to submit to Him and do His will. The end result was that everyone did what was right in their own eyes. As national wealth and security plummeted, people longed for stability and prosperity, setting the stage for the establishment of a monarchy. Samuel's words capture the situation: *"But you have today rejected your God, who Himself saved you from all your adversities and your tribulations; and you have said to Him, 'No, set a king over us!'" (1 Samuel 10:19)*. As born again believers, citizens of Heaven, let us love and submit to God our King.

September 4　　　　　　　　1 Samuel 11, Isaiah 33, Galatians 5

Give it all you've got!

When we pray for the sick, we should give it our all. James tells his readers to, *"Pray for one another, that you may be healed,"* and says that, *"The effectual fervent prayer of a righteous person avails much" (James 5:16)*. The simple advice he gives is as relevant today as it was then. The most effective prayer for healing will be fervent! God does not like anything half-hearted, and prayer is no exception. If we are going to pray, let us do so with all the energy, strength, and vigour that we can muster, determined to get results. This is no place for weak or timid prayers. We are fighting a battle against sickness, and we should mean business, praying as though our life depended on it.

September 5   *1 Samuel 12, Isaiah 34, Galatians 6*

Do not give up

If God blocks your path, give up immediately and repent. Go to Him and He will show you the right way. But if you are on His business, and you face obstacles, do not consider giving up. You need to be strong and push on. God knows that there will be difficult times when we are tempted to give up, which is why Jesus taught that, *"It is always right to pray and not to faint" (Luke 18:1, MKJV).* Success will come, if you persevere in your mission. When troubles come, stand firm and seek God. Listen to Him and let Him strengthen your resolve to continue. Be strong and *very* courageous (Joshua 1:7). As Paul says, *"We should not lose heart in well doing, for in due season we shall reap, if we do not faint" (Galatians 6:9, MKJV).*

September 6   *1 Samuel 13, Isaiah 35, Ephesians 1*

Invest again

Sometimes when the flow of resources dries up in a particular area of our life, it is because God is moving us on. At other times, it is simply because we have stopped investing in that area. If you are currently experiencing a drought in some area of your life, ask God why. If it is because you have stopped investing, start pouring in resources, as God directs. Give to that person or project, and things will start to change. You can invest time, energy, interest, money, materials, prayer, love and care, and see that area start to take off again. Just as God fulfilled His promise in the Holy Land, that, *"The desert shall rejoice and blossom as the rose" (Isaiah 35:1)*, so shall your life blossom abundantly and rejoice, as you invest again!

September 7   *1 Samuel 14, Isaiah 36, Ephesians 2*

Take up your role

You have a role to play on the stage of life, but do you know what it is? No other work can fully satisfy, *"For we are His workmanship, created in Christ Jesus to good works, which God has before ordained that we should walk in them" (Ephesians 2:10).* You need to find your work from God. Listen diligently to Him, and He will begin to show you your true role. God made you and He planned your work. Do not reject this calling, but embrace it wholeheartedly. It is a good work, and as you take it up, He will reveal more of it to you. Step by step you will fulfil your Divine purpose on earth. There is no more glorious life than this. Take up your role and make it your priority today.

September 8   *1 Samuel 15, Isaiah 37, Ephesians 3*

Lay hands on the sick as God directs

Laying hands on the sick is an ancient practice in Christian healing ministry. Touch can be a point of contact through which God's power flows into the body of a sick person. The gospels record how a sick woman touched the hem of Jesus' garment and was fully healed. Jesus knew instantly within Himself that power had gone out of Him (Mark 5:30). You do not have to lay hands on people for them to be healed, but sometimes this is the way God says to do it. It is wise to observe discretion in the use of touch, as it may not always be appropriate. Sometimes it may be best simply to pray. The key, as in every aspect of ministry, is to listen closely to Him and do what He says.

September 9   *1 Samuel 16, Isaiah 38, Ephesians 4*

Follow your spiritual senses

When Samuel chose ancient Israel's second king, his attention was drawn towards a fine looking young man who appeared to be exactly what was needed. But God said, *"Do not look at his appearance or at his physical stature, because I have refused him" (1 Samuel 16:7)*. How important it is that we pay more attention to our spiritual senses than to our physical senses! Many have been fooled by appearances into making decisions that later proved gravely mistaken. The only way to ensure right decision making is to let God guide you. *"For the Lord does not see as man sees; for man looks at the outward appearance, but the Lord looks on the heart" (v.7)*. Seek God and let Him direct you in the decisions you have to make today.

September 10   *1 Samuel 17, Isaiah 39, Ephesians 5*

Be the star that you are

God has made you a star, but are you enjoying your position? You are a unique individual, the only example of you in the universe. No one can be you, let alone be you as well as you can! No one can do all that you can do, in exactly the way that you do it. Embrace your star quality. You are so important to Him that He gave His life for you. When the world makes a star it gives them fame, but when God makes a star He gives them life. The world gives glory for a moment, but God gives life forever. Believe Him when He says He has made you a Priest and a King (Revelation 1:6), a child of light (Ephesians 5:8) shining in the darkness of this world. God has made you a star, so let your light shine today. Be the star that you are!

September 11 *1 Samuel 18, Isaiah 40, Ephesians 6*

Rise up!

When you are feeling weak, stop and wait on God. Isaiah says that, *"Those who wait on the Lord shall renew their strength; they shall rise up with wings like eagles; they shall run and not be weary; they shall walk and not faint" (Isaiah 40:31).* The message is not just that as you worship and seek God your natural energy will be renewed, but that you will be energised by a force beyond yourself, a force so great that it will take you further and higher than you could ever go in your own strength alone. For this reason, waiting on God is not something to leave until things get difficult, but a lifestyle to develop now. Build into your life the discipline of daily seeking God and He will lift you higher than you ever thought possible!

September 12 *1 Samuel 19, Isaiah 41, Philippians 1*

Learn from anger

When David realised that King Saul wanted to kill him, he knew he would have to flee (1 Samuel 19:18). He spoke with his close friend Jonathan, Saul's son, who agreed to check out his father's attitude to David. It soon became clear that David was right. Two days later, during a feast, Jonathan told Saul that David was not able to be present. Saul became very angry, and when challenged by Jonathan over his wish to kill David, Saul cast a spear at him! We can learn a lot from anger. Often it indicates that our aims or expectations are being frustrated. When you next see anger in yourself or others, look to see what goal is being blocked or demand thwarted. Understanding anger is the first step to managing it well.

September 13   *1 Samuel 20, Isaiah 42, Philippians 2*

Don't let negative outcomes stop you

Because we are not healers, our power extends only to prayer. Beyond this point we cannot go. From this point on, what happens is a great mystery to us. There is so much we do not understand about the outcomes in healing ministry. There are times when people recover from conditions that looked sure to kill them, and there are times when people die who looked set to make a full recovery. There are also times when we do everything within our power, medically and spiritually, but the person does not recover. Unless we have settled the limits of responsibility in our hearts, such experiences may shake us. Be clear about your role, and do not let negative outcomes stop you from praying for the sick.

September 14   *1 Samuel 21, Isaiah 43, Philippians 3*

Fly above the storm

If you are a believer, do not be afraid, for God is with you. He says, *"When you pass through the waters, I will be with you" (Isaiah 43:2)*. He is by your side, and you are walking this path together. He knows what you are going through, and understands how you feel. He sees everything, and as you look to Him, He will give you the best possible guidance, so that your foot neither slips nor slides. He knows the way, and will lead you in it. Picture Him and listen, for He will speak with you. Don't project on to Him what you want to hear, but come trusting, with an open and humble heart. Seek truth, for truth alone will free you. Revelation releases. Hear from Heaven, rise up on eagles' wings, and soar above the storm.

September 15   1 Samuel 22, Isaiah 44, Philippians 4

Meditate on these things

At any given moment, we have a choice of how to think. Perhaps the most influential choice we make is between accurate and helpful thinking on the one hand, and unhelpful and inaccurate thinking on the other. It is hard to find a greater statement of this truth than that made by the apostle Paul in his letter to Christians at Philippi: *"Whatever things are true, whatever things are noble, whatever things are just, whatever things are pure, whatever things are lovely, whatever things are of good report, if there is any virtue and if there is anything praiseworthy – meditate on these things"* (Philippians 4:8). Train your mind through practice to think in this way, and the peace of God will fill your heart and mind in Christ Jesus.

September 16   1 Samuel 23, Isaiah 45, Colossians 1

Work from Heaven

Of all the ways in which we may respond to the storms and challenges of life, there is none greater than to wait on the Lord. Isaiah tells us that, *"Those who wait on the Lord shall renew their strength; they shall mount up with wings as eagles; they shall run and not be weary; they shall walk and not faint"* (Isaiah 40:31). As we look to God, we start to be lifted up, whatever the situation. We soar on eagle's wings, rising up above the circumstances, flying above the storm where the air is calm and clear. Waiting on Him we catch the currents of air that lift us, and the higher we fly, the smaller earthly things appear, until we sit with Christ in heavenly places. The best way to view earth is from here! Work from Heaven today.

September 17   *1 Samuel 24, Isaiah 46, Colossians 2*

Look at the fruit

When David was pursued by Saul, he quoted a proverb that was already ancient when he spoke it. He said, *"As the proverb of the ancients says, 'Wickedness proceeds from the wicked'" (1 Samuel 24:13)*. How true this saying is that has stood the test of time and found a place in the Bible. It is the same truth Jesus taught: *"Beware of false prophets, who come to you in sheep's clothing, but inwardly they are ravenous wolves. You will know them by their fruits. Do men gather grapes from thorn bushes or figs from thistles?" (Matthew 7:15,16)*. To know what someone is really like, look at their fruit. But look carefully in the Spirit. Remember that appearances can be deceptive, so that evil may look good, and good can appear evil.

September 18   *1 Samuel 25, Isaiah 47, Colossians 3*

Identify fear as friend or foe

Fear comes in two basic forms. One is a helpful warning system that alerts us to danger. The other is a false alarm that frightens us away from things that are good for us. It is imperative for our well being that we learn to tell the difference. Get it right and you are more likely to survive and grow. Get it wrong and you risk being injured and unfulfilled. People often get it wrong and run from things they need to face. Avoidance is the most common response to anxiety. That may be fine if what you run from is a real threat, but if it is not, you need a different approach. Test your fears today to see whether they are friends or enemies. Learn to flee what you need to flee, and face what you need to face.

September 19   1 Samuel 26, Isaiah 48, Colossians 4

Trust God and be merciful

When fleeing for his life from Saul, David had various opportunities to kill him, but each time he was merciful and let him go. He said, *"The Lord forbid that I should stretch out my hand against the Lord's anointed" (1 Samuel 26:11)*. David's trust was in God, so he left vengeance to Him. The righteous are merciful and show favour. Trust in God enables mercy, because you do not need to settle your own scores. God says of the wicked, *"Vengeance is mine, and recompense; their foot shall slip in due time; for the day of their calamity is at hand, and the things to come hasten upon them" (Deuteronomy 32:35)*. So *"Love your enemies" (Matthew 5:44)* and treat them well. Your love may even challenge some to repent.

September 20   1 Samuel 27, Isaiah 49, 1 Thessalonians 1

Resist the devil's plan for you

Satan will try to stop you fulfilling God's plan for your life. If you diligently seek God and stand firm, resisting Satan in Jesus name, he will ultimately be unable to stop you doing what God has called you to do. However, he may hinder you, just as he hindered the apostle Paul when he endeavoured to visit the Thessalonians. Paul says to them, *"We wanted to come to you – even I, Paul, time and again – but Satan hindered us" (1 Thessalonians 2:18)*. You cannot stop the devil hindering you, but you can stop him wrecking God's plan for your life. Satan can only defeat you if you let him. The moment you seek God, obey His word to you, and resist the devil, he cannot defeat you. Resist him and defeat his plan today!

September 21   1 Samuel 28, Isaiah 50, 1 Thessalonians 2

Use your power for good

It has been said that power corrupts, but the cause is not so much the presence of power but the absence of integrity. Seek God and He will show you how to use your power for good. King Saul repeatedly disobeyed God and lost his reign and his life (1 Samuel 28). King Herod persistently defied God and he too paid with his life. The day came when, *"An angel of the Lord struck him, because he did not give glory to God. And he was eaten by worms and died" (Acts 12:23).* Power is deceptive, often giving an illusion of indestructibility or invincibility. But even a King cannot stand against God. Continued disobedience comes at a high price. Whatever power you have in the lives of others, use it well, as the Lord directs.

September 21   1 Samuel 29, Isaiah 51, 1 Thessalonians 3

Listen carefully to Him

True prosperity starts in the soul and begins at the moment you start to seriously seek God. He says, *"Listen carefully to Me, and eat what is good, and let your soul delight itself in abundance" (Isaiah 55:2).* As you come to Him and hear, your soul is enriched. Prosperity of the soul is the greatest prosperity of all, and the foundation for material prosperity rightly held. Material prosperity may contribute to happiness, but cannot guarantee it. Some are rich and miserable. But a prosperous soul can learn to be content in all things, becoming neither inflated by prosperity, nor deflated by poverty. Prosperity of soul enables you to enjoy wealth and endure lack. Listen carefully, and enjoy true prosperity today.

September 23   1 Samuel 30, Isaiah 52, 1 Thessalonians 4

Press on

Paul says, *"I press toward the goal for the prize of the upward call of God in Christ Jesus"* (Philippians 3:14). There is no greater goal than to know God more closely and obey Him more fully (vv.8-11). At times it may be necessary to pull back from lesser goals, but when it comes to this goal, we should always press forward. Our first priority each day should be to spend time with God, and then work as He directs. No other interest, purpose, or concern should deflect us from our heavenly call. In the words of the hymn writer, *"There's no discouragement will make him once relent, his first avowed intent to be a pilgrim!"* This is our primary purpose in life: *"To know Him and the power of His resurrection!"* (v.10). Press on!

September 24   1 Samuel 31, Isaiah 53, 1 Thessalonians 5

Strengthen yourself in the Lord

Have you been rejected unfairly? Perhaps you made a real contribution, but others were threatened by your influence. Perhaps your motives were misunderstood, and you were wrongly seen as a malefactor rather than a benefactor. Perhaps some did not like you, and wanted you out of the way. All these things happened to Jesus! When you are next rejected, remember that you are in good company. Isaiah says that Christ was, *"Despised and rejected by men, a Man of sorrows and acquainted with grief; and we hid, as it were, our faces from Him; He was despised, and we did not esteem Him"* (Isaiah 53:3). When people turn against you, do what David did. *"David strengthened himself in the Lord his God"* (1 Samuel 30:6).

September 25   *2 Samuel 1, Isaiah 54, 2 Thessalonians 1*

Know that you are loved

You need to be loved. It is one of your deepest needs. Other people may or may not love you, but God's love for you is boundless, deeper than the ocean, higher than the sky, richer than all the wealth of the nations, and purer than the clearest waters. Every moment of each day, He reaches out to you in love. When He died for you, it was for love. When He poured out His Spirit for you at Pentecost, it was for love. When He comes again for you, it will be for love. Everything He does for you is motivated by love, for love is His nature. As John says, *"The one who does not love has not known God. For God is love" (1 John 4:8).* As you seek God, you will come to know that you are loved. Love with His love today.

September 26   *2 Samuel 2, Isaiah 55, 2 Thessalonians 2*

Be sure that the word will find a way

God says of His word: *"It shall not return to Me void, but it shall accomplish what I please, and it shall prosper in the thing for which I sent it" (Isaiah 55:11).* He is working His purpose out as history unfolds. Some people receive His word and follow it, bearing great fruit. Others reject the word, and their lives are fruitless in His sight. But God is never intimidated when His word is blocked. The one who blocks the word will suffer loss, but the One who sent the word will take another way. The word of God has an unerring homing nature, ensuring that it will *always* fulfil its task. As you receive whatever He says to you today, rejoice that whatever the obstacles, the word will find a way.

September 27 2 Samuel 3, Isaiah 56, 2 Thessalonians 3

Enjoy the presence of peace

Jesus said, *"Peace I leave with you, My peace I give to you. Not as the world gives do I give to you. Let not your heart be troubled, neither let it be afraid" (John 14:27)*. Do you see peace as a state you will enjoy when your problems are solved and your difficulties disappear? Whilst this is certainly desirable, there is more to peace than simply the absence of trials. People are sometimes surprised to find that an easy life does not guarantee peace within. Peace is not the absence of problems, but the presence of God. After He rose, Jesus greeted His disciples with the words, *"Peace to you!" (Luke 24:36)*. His presence brings peace. Do not wait for your troubles to cease. Come to Jesus, and enjoy the presence of peace today.

September 28 2 Samuel 4, Isaiah 57, 1 Timothy 1

Give as God directs

Jesus said, *"You have received freely, freely give" (Matthew 10:8)*. Do not be a miser, but give generously as you are prospered and led by God. When you give, do so as God directs. Many give to those who shout the loudest, or make the strongest emotional appeal to their heart. If your giving is guided only by these, it may not be in line with God's will. But if you diligently seek God and follow His guidance, your giving will be most pleasing to Him. Such giving will be fruitful, yielding a great harvest. Give not as man demands, but as God directs. Follow man and you will have man's reward, but give as God directs and you will receive Heaven's reward, a *"good measure pressed down and shaken together" (Luke 6:38)*.

September 29   2 Samuel 5, Isaiah 58, 1 Timothy 2

Guard your heart well

Solomon says, *"Guard your heart with all diligence, for out of it spring the issues of life" (Proverbs 4:23).* Seek to guard your heart against all influences that restrict its capacity to carry God's life to your soul. Toxic attitudes such as self deception and denial can deafen you to God in key areas. Lie to yourself and you close the door to truth in that area, entering a dark place from which the light of reality is banished. If you have closed that door (and all do to some degree, however slight) there is an answer, and it is found in prayer. *"Cleanse me from secret faults"* prayed David (Psalm 19:12). Pray this, and the Holy Spirit will fulfil His promise to lead you into all truth (John 16:13), and the truth will make you free (John 8:32).

September 30   2 Samuel 6, Isaiah 59, 1 Timothy 3

Help the suffering

Fleeing from King Saul, David prayed for deliverance, lamenting that he was a fugitive and social outcast, persecuted by others. He says, *"There is no one who acknowledges me; refuge has failed me; no one cares for my soul" (Psalm 142:4).* God looks for those who will care for the refugees, for the victims of persecution, and for those who are isolated or oppressed. He is angry when, *"Justice is turned back, and righteousness stands afar off; for truth is fallen in the street, and equity cannot enter" (Isaiah 59:14).* Isaiah says, *"The Lord saw it, and it displeased Him that there was no justice. He saw that there was no man, and wondered that there was no intercessor" (Isaiah 59:15b).* Will you be one who stands for others?

OCTOBER

October 1   *2 Samuel 7, Isaiah 60, 1 Timothy 4*

Give what you have

The apostle Paul once wrote to Timothy, a young pastor, with helpful guidance and encouragement, saying, *"Let no one despise your youth, but be an example to the believers in word, in conduct, in love, in spirit, in faith, in purity" (1 Timothy 4:12)*. Encouragement can help us to fulfil our mission in life, but sadly, it is not always given. Each of us has something valuable to give, but do we see it? Perhaps you were never praised for your abilities. Take heart, for God recognises them all, and fully supports you in using those gifts for others. Do not allow lack of human encouragement to hold you back. God is your greatest supporter, and He will back you as you give what you can today.

October 2   *2 Samuel 8, Isaiah 61, 1 Timothy 5*

Trust that God's way for you is the best

We need to know, not only that God is with us, but that He cares for us. Doubt God's care, and you may fail to ask Him for help, or you may question the help He gives. Trust God's care and you are more likely to hear and obey His wise guidance. You may think that you know what is best, but remember that you only see things from an earthly perspective. Your information is limited, whereas He sees all. Trust that He knows what He is doing, and follow His directions. He will guide you in the best possible way. Cling to your own ideas of how things should be, without bringing them into line with His, and you will often be disappointed. Trust God today that His way for you is the best.

October 3   2 Samuel 9, Isaiah 62, 1 Timothy 6

Enjoy what God has given you

Life presents us with many challenges that require our full attention. However, we must beware of becoming more focused on problems and pain than is necessary. Whether we are rich or poor in the things of this world, God, *"Gives us richly all things to enjoy" (1 Timothy 6:17)*. He wants us to enjoy the good things He has given. Some put off enjoyment to a hoped-for future time when they have fulfilled their life goals, but God wants us to enjoy Him and His gifts now. Do not wait to enjoy the good things God has given. You may wait all your life. Stop to enjoy the colour of the sky, the warmth of the sun, the fragrance of a flower. What could you enjoy right now? If there is anything good, enjoy it.

October 4   2 Samuel 10, Isaiah 63, 2 Timothy 1

Yield to the Spirit

There is no greater gift you can give than the gift of yourself. When you put your faith in Christ, God gives you Himself. The Holy Spirit comes and dwells within you. Whatever your human spirit is like, you are given another Spirit. The Holy Spirit does not replace your spirit, but lives with it, seeking to change you so that you become like God, and to empower you to live life to the full. There is no way you could achieve either outcome on your own. Your enemy, the devil, works to steal, kill and destroy, but Jesus works to develop and enable you by His Spirit. This is, *"A spirit of power and of love and of a sound mind" (2 Timothy 1:7)*. Do not give in to fear and anxiety, but yield to the Holy Spirit, and follow Him.

October 5   *2 Samuel 11, Isaiah 64, 2 Timothy 2*

Remember you're accepted

One of the words people least enjoy hearing is *"No."* No one likes to be turned down. The need for acceptance is so strong, and the dislike of rejection so great, that most people will do what they can to be accepted. Some will even compromise their principles and values, in order to gain and maintain acceptance. When we are dependent on others for acceptance, there is always a danger that we may compromise our principles to feel good. But when we make God our primary source of acceptance, we become much less dependent on acceptance by others and much better able to stand for what is right. Remember today that you are accepted in Jesus (Ephesians 1:6), and remain true to yourself and your faith.

October 6   *2 Samuel 12, Isaiah 65, 2 Timothy 3*

Visit God's living library

In giving us the Bible, God has provided us with a living library, inspired by His Spirit (2 Timothy 3:16). The Bible was not created by human beings. People were the writers, but they only wrote what God inspired them to write. The fact that it is 'God-breathed' makes the Bible a living book in a unique sense. When God 'breathed' the Scriptures into existence, He created a library of books, each of which is spiritually alive. The Bible contains more than simply information *about* God - it carries the very *life of* God! When we read its pages and believe, we open a door to Heaven through which God's amazing grace flows freely into our lives. What grace awaits you today?

October 7   2 Samuel 13, Isaiah 66, 2 Timothy 4

Let the record show you walked with God

Jesus said, *"Do not labour for the food that perishes, but for that food which endures to everlasting life, which the Son of Man will give you" (John 6:27)*. What are you working for? Many labour only for the things of this world, giving no thought to eternity. When they die, their estate is given to others, and they take nothing with them but the record of their life. What does your record show? If it shows faith in Christ, sin is covered and eternal salvation assured (Mark 16:16). If it shows good works you will be rewarded (Matthew 10:42). If it shows works that are worthless in God's sight, there will be loss (1 Corinthians 3:15). What will you add to your record today? Walk with God, and labour for lasting rewards.

October 8   2 Samuel 14, Jeremiah 1, Titus 1

Taste and see

There are those who reject God's guidance, and then blame Him when things go wrong. God calls everyone to come to Him, hear, and be blessed. Through Isaiah He says, *"Everyone who thirsts, come to the waters ... Listen carefully to Me and eat what is good ... Hear and your soul shall live" (Isaiah 55:1-3)*. Through the psalmist He says, *"Be still and know that I am God" (Psalm 46:10)*. Christ says, *"Come to Me ... and I will give you rest" (Matthew 11:28)*. There is no greater thing we can do than turn to God and encourage others to do the same. David says, *"Oh taste and see that the Lord is good; blessed is the man who trusts in Him!" (Psalm 34:8)*. Encourage them to taste, because a taste is all it takes to convince.

October 9   2 Samuel 15, Jeremiah 2, Titus 2

Deal with the evils of the day

Jesus said *"Do not be anxious about tomorrow; for tomorrow shall be anxious for its own things. Sufficient to the day is the evil of it"* (Matthew 6:34). Sometimes it is wise to look ahead and prepare for coming challenges, but we need to ensure we do not get anxious trying to sort out tomorrow's problems today. Focus on the real problems of today, rather than on the imagined problems of tomorrow. History records a number of gloomy scenarios predicted by fearful humans that never happened, yet many worried their time away, losing peace, joy, opportunity, and more. Replace anxiety with faith, as you address the evils of today. Minor problems dealt with today may mean disasters averted tomorrow.

October 10   2 Samuel 16, Jeremiah 3, Titus 3

Recognise the universe within

Each of us exists in two worlds: the outer and the inner. The outer world we share with others, but the inner world of the heart is private. From within we manage our lives, directing inner and outer operations. This inner realm is our first country. We may be able to leave a geographical location, but we can never leave ourselves. There is no escaping the inner world. The universe within represents a vast ocean of experience. There is great depth to the human soul. Like the external universe, its furthest reaches are unfathomable by human inquiry. The same awe that we might feel gazing at the stars, can be known by contemplating the vastness of the heavens within. Recognise the universe within you today.

October 11   *2 Samuel 17, Jeremiah 4, Philemon*

First plough your field

It is good to sow seed, but has the field been prepared? We know that seed needs to be sown if there is going to be a harvest, but have we ploughed? To simply scatter seed on the earth is an inefficient and wasteful approach. Much of the seed will be lost. But if we take time to plough first, our yield will be very much greater. What does it mean to plough? It means to prepare the soil for the seed. Someone needs to have prepared the ground. Check that the ground is ready, before you sow your seed. Do not waste your precious seed, by sowing on unploughed soil. Plough and increase your yield! What ground do you need to prepare today? *"Break up your fallow ground and do not sow among thorns"* (Jeremiah 4:3b).

October 12   *2 Samuel 18, Jeremiah 5, Hebrews 1*

Remember your invisible friends

The writer of Hebrews tells us that angels are, *"Ministering spirits sent forth to minister for those who will inherit salvation"* (Hebrews 1:14). When you feel isolated or alone, remember your invisible friends, the angels that surround you on every side. Once upon a time, deep in eternity past, long before the heavens and the earth were formed, our loving Heavenly Father engaged in a sublime act of creation, in which he made a race of eternal beings unique in strength and beauty. This race he called angels. These wonderful beings that work for God and serve His servants, encamp around you, watching over you ceaselessly, day and night. Imagine them now, by your side. Remember your invisible friends.

October 13 *2 Samuel 19, Jeremiah 6, Hebrews 2*

Start the day with Jesus

Jesus said, *"I am with you always" (Matthew 28:20).* When you wake in the morning, who do you see? The writer of Hebrews says, *"But we see Jesus" (Hebrews 2:9).* Develop the habit of looking to your invisible Friend each morning as you awake. There is no better way to start the day than by turning to God. It is said of Moses that, *"By faith he forsook Egypt, not fearing the wrath of the king, for he endured as seeing Him who is invisible" (Hebrews 11:27).* By the same faith you will conquer, looking to Jesus. When you go out, He is with you. When you come in, He is with you. There is never a time when He is not with us. So let us look to Him from the start of each day and *"Run with endurance the race that is set before us" (Hebrews 12:1).*

October 14 *2 Samuel 20, Jeremiah 7, Hebrews 3*

Develop your life management skill

Within yourself you manage great resources. Many different kinds of experience are available to you. You might have an idea, you might attend to data from your physical senses, you might retrieve an event from memory, you might plan, you might reason, and so on. These are just a few of many choices you make as you run your life. How satisfied are you with the way you currently manage your life? The first and greatest management challenge you face is that of managing yourself. Self management is a position into which you are born. You can accept this role and learn to become a good manager, or reject the task and fail in the job. What you cannot do is leave the organisation, because the organisation is you!

October 15 *2 Samuel 21, Jeremiah 8, Hebrews 4*

Take up the sword of the word

"Take ... the sword of the Spirit, which is the word of God" (Ephesians 6:17). With this weapon you will be able to defeat all the lies and temptations of the Evil One. This is how Jesus defeated him in the wilderness, during His temptation. He said each time, *"It is written" (Matthew 4:4,7,10).* We need to know what God says, if we are going to stand. Listen to God and read His word. Know the Scriptures. Then, when your enemy the devil comes, you will be able to completely defeat him. This word is more powerful than any two edged sword (Hebrews 4:12). Take up that sword today, and put the devil to flight. *"Submit to God. Resist the devil and he will flee from you" (James 4:7).*

October 16 *2 Samuel 22, Jeremiah 9, Hebrews 5*

Do God's business

Whoever you are, God has called you into business with Him. If you attend first to His business, all your other business will come right. This requires the discipline of daily listening to God. Each day you will have to fight the temptation to be *too* busy to listen to Him. It is not that busy-ness itself is wrong, but that sometimes we are busy with the wrong things. You have important business to do for Heaven, a unique calling from God. But if you are too busy to listen to Him, your life's work will suffer and you will not fulfil your mission. The most important business of today is your meeting with Him. Make this your first business appointment of each day. God's business awaits you.

October 17   *2 Samuel 23, Jeremiah 10, Hebrews 6*

Commit to becoming who you truly are

Each one of us enters the world with a unique identity or character. This is the true self, the essential person, present from conception. The true self is spiritual and exists forever. However, it may be hidden to a greater or lesser degree. If we lived in a world where from birth onwards we were consistently given accurate information about ourselves, and if we consistently made accurate decisions about ourselves, then, by definition, we would see ourselves as we truly are. But instead of living in that world, we live in one of biased judgements and perceptions, and as a result, the sense of self we develop may be more or less accurate. Listen to God, and He will show you who you really are.

October 18   *2 Samuel 24, Jeremiah 11, Hebrews 7*

You must be born again

The challenge of becoming fully whole is one we are unable to meet unless we experience a radical change of nature. The problem is that in our unredeemed state we cannot see ourselves as we are, having an inherent bias to see things in a distorted way. To see clearly, we must be set free from the corruption that penetrates every fibre of our being, and which blinds us to our true selves. The true self is present within us, but is locked in to the soul, unable to emerge. It must be released if we are going to become who we truly are. We need to experience a spiritual rebirth, in which the true self emerges, and we are freed from the spiritual blindness that prevented us from knowing the truth.

October 19   1 Kings 1, Jeremiah 12, Hebrews 8

Pursue true happiness

Gain something that you value, and you are likely to feel happy. Happiness is a response to real or perceived blessing. Generally, the more we value what is gained, the happier we will be. What is the greatest blessing in life? Jesus' answer is unequivocal: *"Blessed are those who hear the word of God and keep it!" (Luke 11:28).* If you want to be the happiest you can be in this life, this is how to do it: listen to God, believe Him, and do what He says. No greater happiness is possible. In the New Covenant it is easier to do this than ever before. God says, *"I will put My laws in their mind and write them on their hearts" (Hebrews 8:10).* Do not stay unhappy. Pursue true happiness today!

October 20   1 Kings 2, Jeremiah 13, Hebrews 9

Choose God every time

There are those who live in denial concerning the existence of God and Satan. The fact that there is a God and a devil is clearly evident from both the world around us and from the Bible. God is a good God, and He loves you. The devil is a bad devil, and he hates you. God has a plan for your life that will bless you, but Satan wants to destroy you. The choices you make will influence the outcome. You can commit your soul into God's hands, or go your own way and play into the devil's hands. The choice is yours. What will you choose today? Every moment of the day is an opportunity to look to God, hear Him, and follow the guidance of the Holy Spirit. Be one who seizes that opportunity today.

October 21   *1 Kings 3, Jeremiah 14, Hebrews 10*

Move forwards with confidence in God

There is a time for action, but if we are anxious or insecure, we may find it hard to do what is required. The writer to the Hebrews says, *"Do not cast away your confidence, which has great reward" (Hebrews 10:35)*. God wants us to move forwards confidently, and if we are finding it difficult, He will help us. He does this by talking to us in a way that builds our faith. *"Faith comes by hearing, and hearing by the word of God" (Romans 10:17)*. If you are finding it hard to take the next step, go to God and listen. As you wait on Him, His word will strengthen you, so that you reach a place where you have the faith you need to act. You may still feel nervous, perhaps very much so, but conviction will enable you to do what it takes.

October 22   *1 Kings 4, Jeremiah 15, Hebrews 11*

Gather the evidence of faith

Gathering evidence is vital to the success of every enterprise. This is no less true in matters of faith than in other areas. *"Faith is ... the evidence of things not seen" (Hebrews 11:1)*. It is inner evidence, a state of being in which we know in our heart that a thing is so, irrespective of material support. True Bible faith is *not* a matter of convincing oneself. Humans have the capacity to believe all kinds of nonsense! This is not faith, but presumption and delusion. Faith is being convinced by God. It comes out of a relationship with Him, in which He speaks with us. As we hear the word of God, true faith grows, so that we gain a strong inner conviction. Gather faith evidence today, and build something outstanding.

October 23   *1 Kings 5, Jeremiah 16, Hebrews 12*

Run the race of life to win

Watch an athlete being cheered by the crowd as they run to win a race, and you have a clear picture of the strong spiritual support that surrounds *you*, each and every day of your life. The writer of Hebrews says: *"Since we are surrounded by so great a cloud of witnesses, let us lay aside every weight, and the sin which so easily ensnares us, and let us run with endurance the race that is set before us"* (Hebrews 12:1). You are not alone. The saints that have gone before are watching you run. So turn from sin, and give it everything, casting aside all but your calling. If you are listening to God and doing what He says, then you are being cheered on by Heaven. Picture your supporters and imagine their shouts of encouragement!

October 24   *1 Kings 6, Jeremiah 17, Hebrews 13*

Keep your heart right with God

Although He is concerned for your physical health and well-being, it is your heart, the spiritual centre of your soul that matters most to God. He is passionate about every heart and one day He will judge the hearts of all. Contrary to what many believe, the greatest problem of mankind is not environmental but spiritual: our state of heart. God warns through Jeremiah: *"The heart is deceitful above all things and desperately wicked"* (Jeremiah 17:9). We know from the death of Christ that the heart is so corrupt that it is even capable of murdering God. We all need a change of heart, and only God can do that. He promises that if we walk with Him in the light, our hearts will be changed. So stay close to God today!

October 25   *1 Kings 7, Jeremiah 18, James 1*

Aim for Heaven's best

Listen to God, and He will guide you in the best possible path for your life. This is the best by Heaven's reckoning, rather than Earth's. It is an important distinction, as each world has very different criteria for judging value. If you seek mere worldly honour, go your own way, but if you seek God's glory and the best life that Heaven can inspire, listen to the Holy Spirit and He will guide you. Train your spiritual senses to discern between good and evil. Do what God says and you will build with gold, silver, and precious stones, rather than wood, hay, and stubble (1 Corinthians 3:12). When you look back at your life, from the vantage point of the world to come, you will be very glad that you did. Choose Heaven's best.

October 26   *1 Kings 8, Jeremiah 19, James 2*

Choose your defences

Humans need safety and security. Like all creatures, we face various threats, and need to find ways of protecting ourselves against danger, if we are going to survive and thrive. God understands our vulnerability and never condemns us for needing protection. However, the choices we make when it comes to achieving security can create problems for us, some of which extend beyond this life, influencing our eternal destiny. If we trust our own ability, the arm of flesh will fail us (2 Chronicles 32:8), if we trust others, they will let us down (Psalm 146:3), and if we trust riches, they cannot help beyond the grave (Psalm 49:6,7). In Joshua's timeless words, *"Choose this day whom you will serve" (Joshua 24:15).*

October 27 *1 Kings 9, Jeremiah 20, James 3*

Let God chart your course

Your life is like a ship, a fine ocean going vessel. It is designed to make a great voyage, the journey of your life. You are the captain of that vessel and as you take your directions from God today, so the sails will be filled with the wind of the Holy Spirit and you will chart the course that God has planned for you from the beginning. As you say what God says, you will steer your vessel, for the rudder is the tongue (James 3:4,5). By faith you will be able to rest, not only when the sailing is fair, but also during the many storms through which your ship must pass. No man will fully understand the true significance and eternal value of your life's voyage, but the Day of the Lord will declare it.

October 28 *1 Kings 10, Jeremiah 21, James 4*

Resist the devil

From the moment he fell to earth, following his failed attempt to overthrow the Most High, Satan has wrought a trail of devastation in human lives. Robbery, destruction and death are his calling cards. All human suffering and sadness has its source in Satan. When God found evil in him, He purposed to defeat it, and sent His Son to destroy Satan's works: *"For this purpose the Son Of God was revealed, that He might destroy the works of the devil"* (1 John 3:8b). Because of Christ's sacrifice, every one of Satan's activities against us will ultimately be stopped, and he himself will be cast into the lake of fire. The defeat of Satan starts now, as you submit to God and resist Satan. *"Resist the devil and he will flee from you"* (James 4:7).

October 29   *1 Kings 11, Jeremiah 22, James 5*

Anoint with oil as God directs

There may be times when God directs us to anoint a sick person with oil in Jesus' name. James says, *"Is any sick among you? Let him call for the elders of the church, and let them pray over him, anointing him with oil in the name of the Lord"* (James 5:14). Anointing with oil represents an action that may accompany prayer for healing. Like other actions that may be part of Christian healing ministry, such as the laying on of hands or the word of command, anointing with oil should be practised as God directs, and when done in obedience to heaven great works may be wrought. Be ready today, not only to pray for the sick, but also to anoint them with oil, should God so direct.

October 30   *1 Kings 12, Jeremiah 23, 1 Peter 1*

Shatter the rocks

God says through Jeremiah the prophet, *"Is not My word ... like a hammer that breaks the rock in pieces?"* (Jeremiah 23:29). Are you facing situations where you need a breakthrough? If so, go to God and get His word on it. That will do it. Stand on this word and you will prevail. The breakthrough will come. Though it tarry, wait for it. No situation can resist the hammer of God's word. That is why it is so important to hear what God is saying on a daily basis. It is only when we say what God says, that we see Heaven's power. Listen for God's word to you today. It will shatter all the rocks in your life. Some will break faster, others slower, but all will crumble in His time. Alleluia.

October 31   *1 Kings 13, Jeremiah 24, 1 Peter 2*

Reject false guilt

There are two opposite errors into which we may fall when it comes to recognising sin. One is to not see sin where there is sin. The other is to see sin where there is no sin. In this second error, the phenomenon of false guilt, a person thinks they have sinned, and may have guilt feelings, without having actually sinned. False guilt is the emotion you feel when you mistakenly believe that you are wrong. For example, people often adopt goals that God did not set, and then feel guilty when they fail to reach them. When you feel guilty it is important not only to identify the principles you have broken, but to identify whose those principles are. If they are not God's, you need to rewrite them today! Banish false guilt.

NOVEMBER

November 1   *1 Kings 14, Jeremiah 25, 1 Peter 3*

Turn daily to God

Jeremiah says, *"Turn ye again"* *(Jeremiah 25:5)*. The spiritual life is all about turning to God. From first to last, this is the way. Our life should be a continual turning to God. The desperate may turn to God when things look bad, but the wise turn to God at all times. He is your Source, the One who, *"Shall supply all your need according to His riches in glory by Christ Jesus" (Philippians 4:19)*. Only fools fail to look to God. Some will look anywhere but to God, trusting in their own strength or resources, but as the hymn writer says, *"The arm of flesh will fail you!"* There is only one Source on whom we can safely rely. Make God your Source, and turn to Him as often as you can. Turn again!

November 2   *1 Kings 15, Jeremiah 26, 1 Peter 4*

Recognise differences

Despite the obvious evidence of diversity, there is a human tendency to project our own views onto others and to assume that they will think and act like we do. Predictably, such misunderstanding of others leads to all kinds of problems, and often results in deficient and dysfunctional relationships. Do not make the mistake of assuming that the other person will think about things the way you do. They may have a very different outlook. Instead, take the time to find out what they really think. Ask, *"What do you think about that?"* When you know their viewpoint, you will better understand how they feel and what they do. Recognise differences, and build your relationships on reality.

November 3 *1 Kings 16, Jeremiah 27, 1 Peter 5*

Break the spirit of depression

Sometimes depression has a spiritual cause. We live in the middle of a battle that is being waged for human souls. Peter says, *"Your adversary the devil walks about like a roaring lion, seeking whom he may devour" (1 Peter 5:8).* One way he does this is through oppressive influence of a depressive kind. This form of spiritual attack may be experienced despite having both a strong hope and a healthy body! Whenever you discern such attack, both Peter and James say to, *"Resist!" (1 Peter 5:9; James 4:7).* If you submit to God and take your stand against the devil, binding his forces and commanding him to leave in Jesus' name, he will flee from you. In Christ you have the authority to repel his attacks. Use that authority today.

November 4 *1 Kings 17, Jeremiah 28, 2 Peter 1*

Let God make you divine

Christianity is unique amongst world religions, in that no other religion conveys the power to change human nature into divine nature! Only the revelation of Jesus Christ makes total sanctification possible. St Peter says that through the knowledge of Christ, we may become, *"Partakers of the divine nature" (2 Peter 1:4),* whilst St Paul describes how those who look to God, *"Are being transformed into the same image from glory to glory, just as by the Spirit of the Lord" (2 Corinthians 3:18).* Although God works this process in us, He does so, only in response to our desire. God never rapes, He always invites. The humble listener is transformed, whilst the hypocrite remains unchanged.

November 5   *1 Kings 18, Jeremiah 29, 2 Peter 2*

Look again

Once when Elijah prophesied rain, he sent his servant to go and see whether the rain was coming. Six times he sent him to look, and six times the servant returned saying, *"There is nothing" (1 Kings 18:43)*. It was only on the seventh time that the servant saw, *"A cloud, as small as a man's hand, rising out of the sea" (1 Kings 18:44)*. Sometimes when we receive a promise from God, nothing happens for a while, and we may be tempted to think that we got it wrong. But God says to go and look again, and to keep on looking until the promise comes. If He says it will be, it will be! Even when it starts to appear, we may be tempted to doubt, but God turns the small cloud into a mighty storm! Look again today. What do you see?

November 6   *1 Kings 19, Jeremiah 30, 2 Peter 3*

Get ready for the end of the world

People often wonder how and when the world will end. God tells us clearly what will happen. *"The day of the Lord will come as a thief in the night, in which the heavens will pass away with a great noise, and the elements will melt with fervent heat; both the earth and the works that are in it will be burned up" (2 Peter 3:10)*. The end of the world is coming. We do not know when, but we do know how. Are you ready? What if it happened today? Would you be prepared? Do not let that day take you unawares. Saint Peter says, *"Therefore, since all these things will be dissolved, what manner of persons ought you to be in holy conduct and godliness?" (2 Peter 3:11)*. Be ready for the end of the world. Walk in godliness and holy conduct today.

November 7   1 Kings 20, Jeremiah 31, 1 John 1

Walk in the light

John writes, *"If we walk in the light as He is in the light, we have fellowship with one another, and the blood of Jesus Christ His Son cleanses us from all sin"* (1 John 1:7). There is only one antidote to the corrupting effects of sin: the blood of Jesus. No other agent in the universe has this power. Not only does the blood of Christ cleanse us from sin, it cleanses us from *all* sin. As we walk in the light and confess our sins to God, *"He is faithful and just to forgive us our sins and to cleans us from all unrighteousness"* (1 John 1:9). Make it your daily habit to face your sin and turn from it. Come to the light, and the blood will do its wonderful work. The light will reveal your sin and show you how to change your thoughts and actions.

November 8   1 Kings 21, Jeremiah 32, 1 John 2

Ask for help from Heaven

Whether or not you ask others to help you with your problems, it is always right to seek help from God. The psalmist says, *"I will lift up my eyes to the hills – From whence comes my help? My help comes from the Lord, who made heaven and earth"* (Psalm 121:1,2). Lift up your eyes and look to Heaven. Heaven will help you. You will receive the grace you need for whatever situation you are in. God is your Source, your refuge and your strength. Go to Him. He is, *"A very present help in trouble"* (Psalm 46:1b). *"He will not allow your foot to be moved; He who keeps you will not slumber"* (Psalm 121:3). Do not 'go it alone' when you do not have to. Lift up your eyes and seek the Lord. Ask for help from Heaven today.

November 9   1 Kings 22, Jeremiah 33, 1 John 3

Make that call

God makes a great promise when He says through Jeremiah, *"Call to Me, and I will answer you, and show you great and mighty things, which you do not know"* (Jeremiah 33:3). The Lord always answers those who turn to Him in faith. He does not always do so in the way that we expect, but He does always answer. Do not limit God by demanding that He do what you want. Rather, submit to Him, and seek His will. For the plans and purposes of God for you are far greater than any plans you could ever devise for yourself. If you will humbly submit yourself to God and call to Him, He will show you great and mighty things. Do not settle for less when there is more, so much more! God is waiting for you to call today.

November 10   2 Kings 1, Jeremiah 34, 1 John 4

Abide in His love

John writes, *"We have known and believed the love that God has for us. God is love, and he who abides in love abides in God, and God in him"* (1 John 4:16). You need to know and believe the love that God has for you. If you abide in this love, both your nature and your life will be transformed by it. To abide in a place is to stay there. So take time to dwell on the fact that God's love for you is deeper than the ocean, extends further than the most distant galaxy, and is brighter than the most brilliant star. Make it your habit to abide here, for if you stay in love, Love will live in you. Rest in His presence, for He places the highest value on you, accepts you fully, and loves you as the person that you are. Abide in His love today.

November 11   2 Kings 2, Jeremiah 35, 1 John 5

Know that you know

Solomon writes that, *"The spirit of a man is the lamp of the Lord, searching all the inner depths of his heart"* (Proverbs 20:27). God will guide you through an inner witness, if you will heed it. Learn to listen to your spirit, for God will use it to light up your path. Never ignore your 'gut' feelings. There is a level of knowing far deeper than that of the discursive intellect, a quality of knowing that is beyond words. Your human spirit is God's candle. Walk in its light. Follow what you sense in your heart. Choose the prompting of God over the opinions of men. People persuade, but God convicts. This is the knowing of the heart. Practice listening to your spirit and following God's inner witness today.

November 12   2 Kings 3, Jeremiah 36, 2 John

Go with the wind

Jesus said, *"The wind blows where it wishes, and you hear the sound of it, but cannot tell where it comes from and where it goes. So is everyone who is born of the Spirit"* (John 3:8). Do not fight your new nature in God! As a born again believer, your new natural tendency will be to go with the Holy Spirit. The Spirit will prompt you in all kinds of ways. Your old nature will often suggest a different path, and should be resisted. God will guide you, but He will not force you. It is a partnership: you are working together. As you go with the wind of the Spirit, your friendship with God will deepen, and your work will be valuable in the sight of Heaven. Go with the wind today.

November 13 *2 Kings 4, Jeremiah 37, 3 John*

Put your assets to work

The Bible speaks of those that have ears but do not hear (Psalm 115:6; 135:17). It is possible to have resources that we never use. Valuable assets that lie idle will never generate wealth and will in time be lost, which is why Jesus says, *"He who has ears to hear, let him hear!" (Mark 4:9)*. Use it or lose it – that is the message. For those who put their assets to work, more will be generated, but those who fail to manage their assets wisely risk losing even what they had. What resources do you have to use today? Take an inventory. The greatest resource any of us has is the word of God. Seek Him, and put that resource to work. Hear it, accept it, and expect a thirty, sixty, or one hundred-fold return (Mark 4:20).

November 14 *2 Kings 5, Jeremiah 38, Jude*

Follow the spirit of adventure

The Holy Spirit is the Spirit of adventure! King David once said, *"For by You I can run against a troop, by my God I can leap over a wall" (Psalm 18:29)*. With God, ordinary people can do the extraordinary. Barriers to achievement are overcome, obstacles to progress are swept away, and humans do superhuman things, for, *"With God nothing will be impossible" (Luke 1:37)*. When the Spirit gets hold of a person, they rise to unprecedented heights of renown in the sight of Heaven. With God, you *can* do it! There are walls for you to jump, mountains for you to climb, feats and exploits in God! Accept your mission from God today, and set off on your adventure. Heaven is with you!

November 15   2 Kings 6, Jeremiah 39, Revelation 1

Picture Heaven's army

When he saw the size of the Syrian forces that had come to capture his master, Elisha's servant was scared. So Elisha prayed and said, *"'Lord, I pray, open his eyes that he may see.' Then the Lord opened the eyes of the young man, and he saw. And behold, the mountain was full of horses and chariots of fire all around Elisha" (2 Kings 6:17).* Heaven's forces fight for Heaven's objectives. You are surrounded by angels on every side, invisible soldiers from Heaven. Day and night they work on your behalf, fighting to fulfil God's purpose in your life. Angels are fighting for you today, powerful secret forces. Picture Heaven's army gathered with you, and let faith arise in your heart.

November 16   2 Kings 7, Jeremiah 40, Revelation 2

Follow God's timing

Timing is important. *"To everything there is a season, a time for every purpose under heaven" (Ecclesiastes 3:1).* How do you get your timing right? There is a time to wait and a time to act. Waiting enables you to prepare and be ready to 'catch the tide', whilst action enables you to seize the moment. But how do you know when to wait and when to act? The key is to follow God's guidance. As you listen to Him each day, He will tell you what you need to know, and His Spirit will prompt you in what to do, and when to do it. Like the lepers at the gate who asked, *"Why sit we here until we die?" (2 Kings 7:3),* you will know when the waiting time is over and it is time for decisive action. Follow God's timing today.

November 17   *2 Kings 8, Jeremiah 41, Revelation 3*

Build on the rock

There is only one way to build anything of true significance in life. Jesus taught that only the works of those who listen to Him and do what He says will remain (Matthew 7:24-27). What have you built, and on what is it founded? Is your house built on the rock of God's word to you, or on the shifting sands of your own ideas and desires? This is a question you should regularly ask yourself. If you find that you are building on the rock, you have something to celebrate, but if you find that you have built on the sand, you have an opportunity to repent and move your faith and your works to solid ground. By doing the works of God you will enjoy the deepest peace, and be ready for the return of Christ.

November 18   *2 Kings 9, Jeremiah 42, Revelation 4*

Seek God and grow

Spiritual rebirth is the first step to becoming who we truly are. None can become fully whole without coming into a personal relationship with God. The realisation of the true self is a journey of self discovery and transformation that starts here. Self realisation is the process by which we progressively become who we were made to be. It is a developmental path. The true self is released through new birth, but like a physical infant, the spiritual baby needs to grow. Spiritual nurture is essential for healthy spiritual growth. Just as a human mother may love and care for her baby God nurtures His children. As you seek God and hear Him you are fed with spiritual food from heaven. God's word is food. Seek Him and grow today.

November 19   2 Kings 10, Jeremiah 43, Revelation 5

Let the light of hope burn brightly

Never give up hope in God. When the light of hope goes out, it is often replaced by the darkness of grief, depression or despair. Put your trust in God, for hope abounds where faith is strong, as Paul's prayer for the Romans demonstrates: *"Now may the God of hope fill you with all joy and peace in believing, that you may abound in hope by the power of the Holy Spirit" (Romans 15:13)*. You cannot fill yourself with joy and peace, but you can believe. Listen to God and believe what He says to you. Whatever the situation, believe that He is working for your good in it. Diligently seek God, and you will come to see things from His perspective. Though the light may be dim on earth, it is always bright in Heaven.

November 20   2 Kings 11, Jeremiah 44, Revelation 6

Use the power God has given you

Having led Israel out of Egypt, Moses faced a desperate situation at the Red Sea, with Pharaoh and his armies behind him, and impassable mountains on either side. At that moment he did what people often do at such times: he cried out to God in prayer. *"Well done!"* you might say, but you would be wrong. God's response was to rebuke Moses. He said, *"Why do you cry to Me? Tell the children of Israel to go forward. But lift up your rod and stretch out your hand over the sea and divide it" (Exodus 14:15,16)*. This was not an act for God to perform, but an act for Moses to believe for. Do not ask *God* to do what He has asked *you* to do. Use the power God has given you today.

November 21   2 Kings 12, Jeremiah 45, Revelation 7

Don't judge by appearances

When things look bad, it is more important than ever to view them from Heaven. Earth affords a particular view, but it is not the full picture. Some contemporary physicists tell us there may be at least 11 dimensions to the universe. There is so much we do not see, so it is imperative that we find a way of transcending the limitations of our human senses. Prayer provides the missing information we need. When things seem to be going wrong, remember that there are things you cannot see. What may look like impending defeat is not necessarily so. Instead of judging by appearances, look to God and get His perspective on it. He will show you the true state of things, and the steps you need to take.

November 22   2 Kings 13, Jeremiah 46, Revelation 8

Don't walk alone

It is said of many in the Bible that they walked with God. There is no need to face life alone. Jesus is by your side, walking with you as a friend. Let your friend support you through the good times and the bad. Consult Him often, and let Him inform and advise you on every matter. Together you will always find the best way through. There may be times when you are on your own, humanly speaking, but you cannot be separated from Him. He is there by your side. Remember this and turn to Him. Draw on His strength, trust in His love, and listen to His words. He is with you as a friend, a good friend, the most faithful friend you will ever have. Trust in His friendship today. Don't walk alone.

November 23   2 Kings 14, Jeremiah 47, Revelation 9

Put first things first

When walking with God is our first priority, everything else falls into place. Jesus said, *"Seek first the kingdom of God and His righteousness, and all these things shall be added to you"* (Matthew 6:33). Take care not to neglect your relationship with God. Walking with Him is the most important thing you can do in life. We will all be tempted to focus more on the gifts than on the Giver. There are so many needs and concerns that clamour for our attention, and when we pour all our energy into meeting these, we become like those who build the walls of a house before they have built the foundations. Sooner or later, the walls will fall. This is a temptation to continually resist. Seek God first and your house will be strong in Him.

November 24   2 Kings 15, Jeremiah 48, Revelation 10

Take the time to understand

Take the time to understand others. Make the effort to work them out. Because people are often hard to understand, we may be tempted to not make that effort. The heart might be compared to a deep well. Solomon says, *"Counsel in the heart of man is like deep water, but a man of understanding will draw it out"* (Proverbs 20:5). Imagine you are standing by that well. You must lower your bucket to draw water. The bucket will not rise and fall without assistance. You must keep lowering the bucket until you reach the water, and you may have to go deeper than you think. The purposes of the heart are like that, but an understanding person will draw them out. Let God give you that understanding. Take the time to understand.

November 25   *2 Kings 16, Jeremiah 49, Revelation 11*

Be ready for the Judgement

A time is coming when seven trumpets will sound in Heaven. The sound of each heralds a key event at the close of human history, events that culminate in Christ conquering the kingdoms of this world. Jesus will reign over all: *"And He shall reign forever and ever!" (Revelation 11:15)*. All the dead will be judged on that day. For those who love God and do good it will be a glorious day. Prophets, saints, and all those who fear the name of the Lord, however small or great, will be rewarded. But for those who persist in rejecting God and doing evil, it will be a dark day of separation from all that is good. Be ready for the Last Judgement. Believe in Christ, and obey Him. Do as much good as you can!

November 26   *2 Kings 17, Jeremiah 50, Revelation 12*

Cultivate a life of prayer

There may be many things that clamour for your attention today. Your task is to manage them prayerfully, rather than have them manage you. When life gets busy, see it is an opportunity to practise keeping your eyes on God. In all you do, look to God and let Him guide you. Little by little, you will learn how to be involved in life's activities whilst, *"Praying always with all prayer and supplication in the Spirit" (Ephesians 6:18)*. This is the way: a life of prayer. Remember Enoch, who walked with God. Keep your heart open to Him, and He will guide you through each day. Let Him direct you from Heaven, so that you do the works of Heaven on earth and fulfil your holy calling. Cultivate a life of prayer.

November 27   2 Kings 18, Jeremiah 51, Revelation 13

Examine yourself before God

Self realisation begins with spiritual rebirth and develops as we seek God daily. We grow as we look to Him. The Holy Spirit progressively transforms us so that we become increasingly like Christ in our own nature, whilst retaining our own distinctive identity. Personal relationship with God is the setting for true personal development. It is the safest and most effective context for self examination and the revelation of things we do not see, providing the security we need if we are going to face potentially threatening facts about ourselves. The sure foundation for self examination is Divine contemplation. Reflect on yourself in the Light, that your life may be changed for the better today.

November 28   2 Kings 19, Jeremiah 52, Revelation 14

Let God direct you in difficulty

What do you do, when you cannot see a way forward, or a way out of the difficulties you are in? If you panic and make an ill-judged response, you may make things worse, but if you still your soul and seek God, you will find both the direction and the strength that you need. However difficult, desperate, or dangerous the situation is, God has got a path for you to take in it. But the only way you will discover that path is by looking and listening to Him. In terms of its eternal value, this path will be the best one you could possibly take in that situation. Take it, and you will make it. The full support of Heaven is given to those who serve Heaven's King. Let God direct you in difficulty.

November 29   2 Kings 20, Lamentations 1, Revelation 15

Face your giants by faith

What do you do when you face something or someone bigger than you? The Bible contains many stories of those who faced insurmountable obstacles and powerful enemies. For Moses there was the Red Sea (Exodus 14), for Shadrach, Meshach and Abednego there was the fiery furnace (Daniel 3), and for David there was Goliath (1 Samuel 17). When you face your Goliath, remember that God has already prepared you by building your faith to the point where you are now ready to face this challenge. It will not be easy, but if you draw on the faith that you have and follow God's directions, you *will* overcome. What has God called you to face today? Do not run from it. Run to God and He will show you what to do.

November 30   2 Kings 21, Lamentations 2, Revelation 16

Strive together in prayer

Some things are best done alone, but others require that we work together. The best teamwork is built on prayer. When each member prays for the others, great things may be accomplished. Paul had no hesitation in asking others to join him in fervent intercession for the success of his work. He writes, *"Now I beg you, brethren, through the Lord Jesus Christ, and through the love of the Spirit, that you strive together with me in prayers to God for me" (Romans 15:30).* Be like him, and boldly ask for prayer. Pray for those in any way related to your life's work, and have them pray for you. Outstanding things happen when one person obeys God, but when people strive together, the results are often even more remarkable.

December

December 1   2 Kings 22, Lamentations 3, Revelation 17

Check your dependency

Self awareness is a valuable personal quality, but why? Some will answer *"To become more whole"*, others, *"To advance my career"*, or, *"To build better relationships."* Whilst these may be valid aims, none expresses the true purpose of self examination. Jeremiah writes, *"Let us search out and examine our ways, and turn back to the Lord"* (Lamentations 3:40). He knew that the great purpose of self examination is to check our dependency. We examine ourselves daily to see where we have misplaced our faith by trusting in someone or something more than God. Then we turn back to the Lord our Source, from whom all blessings flow. Check your dependency each day.

December 2   2 Kings 23, Lamentations 4, Revelation 18

Stay your mind on God

In a world of stress and anxiety, peace is freely available to all. Isaiah says, *"You will keep him in perfect peace, whose mind is stayed on You, because he trusts in You"* (Isaiah 26:3). Make faith the foundation and the focus of your mind. As the foundation, trust in God will support you through the good times and the bad. As the focus, it will keep you in the centre of His will. Stay your mind on Him, and He will guide you, open doors to you, and enable you to fulfil your calling. Only God can give you the wisdom you need to make the right choices. He will speak to you, and His Holy Spirit will witness to your spirit when to go, and when to stop. Seek Him today and proceed with peace of heart and mind.

December 3   2 Kings 24, Lamentations 5, Revelation 19

Go and look

When you lose something, do you not go and look for it? You do not wait for it to pop up and say, *"Here I am."* Jesus said, *"Seek and you shall find" (Matthew 7:7)*. Seeking is the key to discovery and development. Fail to seek and you will be stuck with what you have. This is the default option. But start seeking and you will discover more. It is good that we learn to be content *in* any situation, but it is not good to be content *with* every situation. Rise up and seek change where change is required. Pursue it with passion. What should you seek? Decide now, and prayerfully plan a definite practical step that you will take today towards obtaining what is needed. Do not wait for it to come to you. Go and look for it.

December 4   2 Kings 25, Ezekiel 1, Revelation 20

Overcome by faith

Planet Earth is a spiritual war zone, where two armies are locked in mortal combat: the army of God and the army of Satan. This battle will continue until Christ returns. That Day will change everything. Satan will be bound for a thousand years, after which he will be loosed again for a short time, before being thrown into the lake of fire forever (Revelation 20:2-10). Evil will then be finally defeated. Until then, God calls us to, *"Fight the good fight of faith" (1 Timothy 6:12)*, for it is by faith we overcome. *"For whatever is born of God overcomes the world. And this is the victory that has overcome the world – our faith. Who is he who overcomes the world, but he who believes that Jesus is the Son of God" (1 John 5:4&5)*.

December 5   *1 Chronicles 1, Ezekiel 2, Revelation 21*

Lift your eyes to Heaven

There are moments in life when we glimpse eternity, moments when our hearts are touched, and for a time the veil between this world and the next is taken away. Oh the beauty of those moments. It is indescribable. Words cannot capture it. Something happens in the heart at such times. We are touched and changed forever, in a moment of time that we will never forget. These are the memories on which to feed, for they speak of a place that can only be reached by love, a world in which God shall wipe away every tear and there shall be no more death, neither sorrow, nor crying, neither shall there be any more pain: for the former things are passed away (Revelation 21:4).

December 6   *1 Chronicles 2, Ezekiel 3, Revelation 22*

Drink from the river

At the conclusion of the great vision he received on the Isle of Patmos, John sees a beautiful river flowing from the throne of God: *"And he showed me a pure river of water of life, clear as crystal, proceeding out of the throne of God and of the Lamb ... On either side of the river, was the tree of life, which bore twelve fruits, each yielding its fruit every month: and the leaves of the tree were for the healing of the nations"* (Revelation 22:1,2). This river flows into the life of everyone who believes. Whoever trusts in Jesus, receives the river and the overflowing abundant life it brings. There is no river like it on earth. Its crystal clear waters cleanse, refresh and renew us. Its life heals nations. All we need do is turn to God in faith. The river will do the rest.

December 7   *1 Chronicles 3, Ezekiel 4 & 5*

Submit your will to His

Jesus teaches us to pray, *"Your will be done on earth, as it is in Heaven" (Matthew 6:10b)*. God loves people and wants to bless them, but there is a problem. Many people, even believers, will not listen to Him. As a result they miss out on God's best. Wanting their own way, they do their own thing, rather than seek God and do His will. Because He loves them, God gets very upset by this. Check daily to ensure that you are listening to Him and following His directions. Human good ideas are not good enough. God sees the whole universe at a glance. Can you? Without Him, even our best decisions are made on the basis of inadequate data, but with Him, even the fool becomes wise. Submit your will to His today.

December 8   *1 Chronicles 4, Ezekiel 6 & 7*

Reach out and touch the Lord

On one occasion when a sick woman touched the edge of Jesus cloak, power immediately went out from Him and she was healed (cf. Luke 8:43-48). Whenever we make a connection with God, Heaven's transforming power flows in our life. Connecting with Him is so easy that even a small child can do it. It is simply a matter of coming to Him in faith. Faith makes the connection. It is like turning on a light. You flick the switch, the connection is made, and electricity flows. God speaks, giving us the switch of faith, but we still need to flick it. When we come to Him with an open and believing heart, power flows through from Heaven and changes things. Flick the switch today. Reach out and touch the Lord.

December 9   *1 Chronicles 5, Ezekiel 8 & 9*

Discover your hidden sins

Jesus promised that we would find freedom by knowing the truth. But when it comes to knowing the truth about ourselves we face a serious problem, for as Jeremiah says, *"The heart is deceitful above all things, and desperately wicked; who can know it? I, the Lord, search the heart, I test the mind, even to give every man according to his ways, according to the fruit of his doings" (Jeremiah 17:9,10).* We can never know ourselves by self examination alone. Our personal biases and blind spots are too great. But God, who sees all, offers to help us. *"Abide in My word"* says Jesus, and, *"You shall know the truth" (John 8:31,32).* Listen to Jesus, and He will show you your hidden sins, that you may be free!

December 10   *1 Chronicles 6, Ezekiel 10 & 11*

Be honest with God

Amongst those who claim to be mind readers, some infer thoughts from psychological clues such as body language, whilst others try to see using occult means. But not one of them can directly read the mind of another. God, on the other hand, hears everything, not just the words we speak to others, but what we say in our hearts. He says, *"I know the things that come into your mind" (Ezekiel 11:5).* Every one of your thoughts is known to Him. Those who plan evil, believing that God does not see, are fooling themselves. God knows exactly what they think. But those who do good can rejoice, because they are known by God. He knows how you feel and He knows what you think, so you can be completely honest with Him.

December 11   *1 Chronicles 7, Ezekiel 12 & 13*

Open your eyes

How clearly do you see? During His earthly ministry Christ opened the eyes of the physically and the spiritually blind. Both are life changing. Just as the restoration of physical sight enables us to enjoy the light of earth, so the opening of our spiritual eyes enables us to see by Heaven's light. Jesus said, *"Unless a man is born again, he cannot see the kingdom of God" (John 3:3b).* When you put your faith in Christ, you were born a citizen of Heaven, so open your eyes and walk in the light. All of us have blind spots, but they need not remain. Look to God, and He will show you the truth that you need to see. Exchange ignorance for knowledge, and self-deception for self-awareness. Keep your spiritual eyes open today.

December 12   *1 Chronicles 8, Ezekiel 14 & 15*

Seek Him early and often

Jesus says, *"Come to Me, all you who labour and are heavy laden, and I will give you rest" (Matthew 11:28).* God is ever calling everyone on earth to come to Him, for He longs deeply to enjoy our friendship. In this world we will have stress, but in His presence we will find eternal peace. When we come to Him, He speaks with us and shows us the way. He is always ready to talk to you, so do not hold back, do not hesitate. Come now. The wise make listening to God the first thing they do each day. There is no better way to live than to seek Him early and often. Each time you come to Him, you will be refreshed, strengthened, and taken forwards. Come often into His presence, for there is no better way.

December 13   *1 Chronicles 9, Ezekiel 16 & 17*

Invest in people

Relationships are one of the greatest sources of upset and hurt. People want good relationships, but they are not always prepared to do what it takes to build them. To some extent good relationships are a choice that we make. We cannot guarantee that we will get on well with others, as they may dislike or oppose us, however good we are to them. But we *can* choose to treat others well, with compassion and integrity. The apostle Paul writes, *"If it is possible, as much as depends on you, live peaceably with all men"* (Romans 12:18). Peace with all should be our aim. Think of your relationships. Are there any in which you have not invested as you ought? If so, act today, and give that relationship a chance.

December 14   *1 Chronicles 10, Ezekiel 18 & 19*

Get a new heart

Ezekiel says, *"Cast away from you all the transgressions which you have committed, and get yourselves a new heart and a new spirit"* (Ezekiel 18:31). His words capture the truth that repentance is more than a change of behaviour. A person may change what they do, but their heart may not change. In such cases they might look good outwardly, but inwardly it is a mess. This was the state of the scribes and Pharisees whom Jesus condemned (Matthew 23:27). They were pretending to be spiritual. True repentance is a change of heart and mind. We turn to God, giving Him His rightful throne in our heart, and He gradually changes us into His own image. Do not try to beautify the old heart. Get yourself a new one.

December 15   *1 Chronicles 11, Ezekiel 20 & 21*

What's the name of your castle?

Your innermost being, the essential you or true self, is vulnerable and requires protection in a fallen world. Born into an environment of uncertainty and insecurity, we guard ourselves against emotional pain by raising inner defences, building a fortress for the soul in which we hope we will be safe, and from which we will direct our life. This inner castle is our refuge in which we trust. Where do you run for safety? *Wealth, Poverty, Power, Influence, Beauty, Fame, Intellect, Dominance, Submission, Withdrawal, Helplessness,* and *Avoidance,* are just a few examples of such castles. What is the name of yours? Only one name signifies spiritual and psychological health: *The Name of the Lord* (Proverbs 18:10).

December 16   *1 Chronicles 12, Ezekiel 22 & 23*

Pray for your nation

Your country needs your prayers. God looks to see who is praying for their nation. Praying for our country is always important, as it shapes the national destiny. Nations that turn from God are at particular risk, and are in special need of intercession. Such was Israel in the days of the prophet Ezekiel. The extent of their degeneration is reflected in God's words to him: *"So I sought for a man among them who would make a wall, and stand in the gap before Me on behalf of the land, that I should not destroy it; but I found no one"* (Ezekiel 22:30). When God looks at your prayers and mine, does He find prayer for our nations? It is time to 'stand in the gap' before God on behalf of the land! Your prayers can change nations.

December 17   *1 Chronicles 13, Ezekiel 24 & 25*

Leave vengeance to God

Unlike human vengeance, God's judgements are an expression of His love, designed to restore Divine order and bring justice to all. Time and again, God says through Ezekiel that His judgements are done so that *"They shall know that I am the Lord"* (e.g. Ezekiel 25:.5,7,11,17). God wants us to know Him, turn from our own ways and choose His way. He says, *"Be still and know that I am God"* (Psalm 46:10), and if we choose this path, we will have nothing to fear. But those who reject God and His directions *will* be judged. Judgement stops that person or nation from further fulfilling their evil plans, and shows them who is God. Oppose evil today, but out of love rather than vengeance.

December 18   *1 Chronicles 14, Ezekiel 26 & 27*

Make God your financial adviser

In chapter 27 of his book, the prophet Ezekiel describes the great prosperity of the ancient city of Tyre, and prophesies its destruction. The end of Tyre was just as he predicted. In Ezekiel's day the people of Tyre dwelt secure, strong in the confidence that their remarkable prosperity provided. Little did they realise that the foundation of their faith was no more than shifting sand. Like all those who trust in riches, their security was utterly destroyed, leaving them with nothing. Had they sought true riches, the knowledge and guidance of God, all they needed would have been given them, but they chose the fading glory of this world, and doomed themselves to certain loss. Make God your financial adviser today!

December 19   *1 Chronicles 15, Ezekiel 28 & 29*

Be your own friend

A good self relationship is fundamental to abundant living. If you have put your faith in Jesus, God has accepted you (Ephesians 1:6). So now you should accept yourself. As your own enemy, you will be divided in yourself, and your health, happiness, and achievement may be compromised. But be your own friend, and you are more likely to look after yourself properly. How would you describe your relationship with yourself? Listen to your own self talk. If someone else spoke to you like that, how would you feel? The way to build a good self relationship is the same as building a friendship with someone else. Be friendly! Do not deny your faults and failings, but be your own friend today.

December 20   *1 Chronicles 16, Ezekiel 30 & 31*

Do all things by prayer

Saint Paul advises, *"In everything by prayer and supplication, with thanksgiving, let your requests be made known to God" (Philippians 4:6)*. Let an attitude of prayer pervade all you do. Involve God in your internal conversations. Include Him in your personal and business decision making. Seek His opinions before you seek the opinions of others. Share your joys with Him, and let Him in to your pain and grief. He is your constant companion, your invisible Guide. If you will humble yourself before Him and listen, He will lead you in the way that is right for you. Seek Him in all things, consult Him at every stage, and He will keep you in perfect peace. Let your motto be, *"All things by prayer!"*

December 21   *1 Chronicles 17, Ezekiel 32 & 33*

Blow the trumpet

Ezekiel says that the duty of a watchman is to blow the trumpet whenever he sees a foreign army coming against the land (Ezekiel 33:3). What do you do when you see that another person or group of people is in danger? You have a choice: keep quiet or blow the trumpet. We should always do what we can, but exactly how we respond must be informed by the guidance of the Holy Spirit. When it is right to blow the trumpet, we should ensure that the warning we send is a clear one. Saint Paul says, *"For if the trumpet makes an uncertain sound, who will prepare for battle?"* (1 Corinthians 14:8). Do you have a warning to give? If so, seek God today and let Him show you how to best deliver your message.

December 22   *1 Chronicles 18, Ezekiel 34 & 35*

Make Jesus your pastor

Ezekiel asks, *"Should not shepherds feed the sheep?"* (Ezekiel 34:2). Earthly shepherds will fail, but not the Good Shepherd, so make Him your pastor. Jesus' sheep hear His voice and follow Him. He knows each one personally, and calls them by name. As one of His sheep, you need not fear. He will always feed you, for He is the Good Shepherd. Come to Him now. He alone will satisfy the deepest longing of your heart. He alone will teach you perfect doctrine. He alone will direct your path accurately. He alone will bless you richly. He alone will give you supernatural grace in your trouble and distress. No earthly shepherd can compare. You have the Pastor that you need, and His name is Jesus. Feed from His hand today.

December 23 *1 Chronicles 19, Ezekiel 36 & 37*

Thank God for His undeserved blessings

God says to Israel through Ezekiel that He will multiply the fruit of their trees and the increase of their fields (Ezekiel 36:30). However, He makes it clear that He will do this, not because it is deserved, but for the sake of His holy name (vv.21,22). Their ways have been evil (v.31), but God says, *"I will cleanse you from all your filthiness" (v.25), "I will give you a new heart and put a new spirit within you" (v.26). "I will put My Spirit within you and cause you to walk in My statutes, and you will keep My judgements and do them" (v.27). "You shall be My people, and I will be your God" (v.28).* None of us deserve God's blessing. The Bible says that we have all sinned. But Jesus died so that we might receive God's undeserved blessing.

December 24 *1 Chronicles 20, Ezekiel 38 & 39*

Thank God for a perfect body

The body is an amazing miracle of creation. Its complex mechanisms, sophisticated systems, and cellular variety, all proclaim the Creator's intelligent design. *"Fearfully and wonderfully made,"* says the Psalmist, in awe before the representation of God. Saint Paul calls this body it a 'tent' because, despite its glory, it is a temporary dwelling to be superseded by the eternal body we will receive at the Resurrection. If the present body is glorious, the heavenly body will be far more so. Look after your 'tent' – it is the only one you have down here on earth! But do not spend more time lamenting lost youth and beauty than celebrating the perfect body you will enjoy forever. The best is yet to come.

December 25   *1 Chronicles 21, Ezekiel 40 & 41*

Receive gifts every day

At Christmas it is traditional to give gifts. These are often wrapped, creating a sense of mystery and an element of surprise when they are opened. For the Christian, the gifts of Christmas Day are a symbol of God's gifts to us, including the greatest gift of all: the gift of His Son. Jesus taught us to pray, *"Give us this day our daily bread" (Matthew 6:11)*. Each day, He gives us new gifts to unwrap, fresh expressions of His love. What are your presents from God today? Each morning you can be like a child on Christmas day, so keen to open your presents that everything else must wait! Why not start each day with excitement at the thought of God's presents to you? What heavenly gifts will you unwrap today?

December 26   *1 Chronicles 22, Ezekiel 42 & 43*

Feed on God's word

When Satan tempted Him to put food before God, Jesus replied, *"Man shall not live by bread alone, but by every word that proceeds from the mouth of God" (Matthew 4:4)*. He knew that there was only one way to satisfy the deepest hunger of the human heart, and that none of this world's pleasures could ever fully satisfy it. Where do you go to meet your deepest need? Jesus told his hearers to work for lasting satisfaction rather than passing pleasures. He said, *"Do not labour for the food which perishes, but for the food which endures to eternal life, which the Son of Man will give you" (John 6:27)*. First put your energy into seeking God. His words alone will satisfy the hunger of your heart and quench the thirst of your soul.

December 27 *1 Chronicles 23, Ezekiel 44 & 45*

Make your choices with God

The power to choose is one of the most fundamental human capacities. God created both angels and humans with such great freedom of choice that they could even choose to reject their Creator. Every waking moment is a moment of choice. Whether young or old, rich or poor, slave or free, choice remains. How are you using your power to choose? Reflect for a moment on some of the choices you have made. How constructive do you feel these were? If you could go back and do things differently would you? We may not always be able to undo the effects of bad choices, but we can learn from them for the future. What good lessons have you learnt from the bad choices you have made? Put them to work today.

December 28 *1 Chronicles 24, Ezekiel 46 & 47*

Look up

People often look downwards when they are struggling with problems and difficulties, but the writer of Psalm 121 says, *"I will lift up my eyes to the hills – from whence comes my help? My help comes from the Lord, who made heaven and earth" (vv.1,2)*. He knew that the answer was not down on the ground, but up in God's Heaven. When times are hard you need to look upwards, not downwards. Keep your eyes raised, *"Looking unto Jesus, the author and finisher of our faith, who, for the joy that was set before Him endured the cross, despising the shame, and has sat down at the right hand of the throne of God" (Hebrews 12:2)*. Look to Jesus, and you will make it. He will complete His work in you. Whatever you face today, look up.

December 29   *1 Chronicles 25, Ezekiel 48*

Get in the flow of wealth

When life is easy and wealth abounds, the mean keep tight hold of their riches, but when life is hard and things are in short supply, the generous keep on giving. Generosity has little to do with wealth. Both billionaires and beggars may be generous or greedy. It is a choice we make, a choice that activates spiritual laws and which redirects the flow of wealth. We choose to give and grow, or to withhold and wither! King Solomon, the wealthiest man of his time, said, *"There is one who scatters, yet increases more; and there is one who withholds more than is right, but it leads to poverty. The generous soul will be made rich, and he who waters will also be watered himself" (Proverbs 11:24,25)*.

December 30   *1 Chronicles 26 & 27*

Pray it through

The most effective prayers are those inspired by God. Hearing from Heaven is no luxury for the Christian, but a basic necessity of spiritual life. Practice listening to God as you pray, and letting God direct your prayer. Look to Him, and pray as He leads you. Gradually, you will reach a point where you sense that you have prayed everything God wants you to pray at this stage. At this point you may get a sense in your spirit that *"It's done."* That is the time to stop, not before. When the impetus to pray that comes from Heaven ceases, you have completed your work for the moment, and it is time to take a break. This is what it means to 'pray it through'. Do not leave the job half done. Pray it through today.

December 31 				*1 Chronicles 28 & 29*

Remember who is with you

Jesus said, *"I am with you always" (Matthew 28:20).* When times are hard, remember that you are with the God who will *"Make a road in the wilderness and rivers in the desert" (Isaiah 43:19).* Jesus, your Friend, is with you, walking by your side, and working for your good. Paul says, *"We know that all things work together for good to those who love God, to those who are called according to His purpose" (Romans 8:28, MKJV).* God will make a way. Trust Him in this, and stand firm. As you look to Him, He will give you the strength, the grace, the guidance - whatever you need to get through. You are not walking this path alone, but you are walking it together with God. Let your Friend support you all the way.

www.ingramcontent.com/pod-product-compliance
Lightning Source LLC
Chambersburg PA
CBHW030410100426
42812CB00028B/2907/J